Britain's Haunted Heritage

Britain's
Haunted Heritage

KEITH B. POOLE

MAGNA
BOOKS

First published in 1988 by Robert Hale Ltd

© Keith B. Poole 1988

This edition published 1995 by
The Promotional Reprint Company Ltd,
exclusively for Magna Books, Magna Road,
Wigston, Leicester LE18 4ZH

ISBN 1 85422 903 6

Printed and bound in Finland

Contents

Introduction 9
1 East Anglia 13
2 The Home Counties 26
3 The Heart of England 50
4 The North 77
5 The South East 101
6 The South West 118
7 Scotland 157
8 Wales 171
Principal Sources 181
Acknowledgements 183
Index 185

For
Madeline

Introduction

In spite of modern education and in a highly technical age dominated by computers, ghost stories continue as they have done since the beginning of time. They are the last-surviving and integral part of the legends and folklore which formed the foundations of British heritage. Ghosts have been sketched, photographed, struggled with and attacked, have brought warnings of death and even been shot at. Thousands of people have never seen a ghost nor ever believed in their existence. Those who have, accept them. Even people with scientific and logical minds have found their rational thinking challenged and defeated, often agreeing 'there must be something' when disturbed by a manifestation they were unable to analyse.

As Christina Hole, that indisputable scholar and writer of ghost lore, pointed out in *Haunted England*, 'a house that is reputed to be haunted is often difficult to let', and legal action has been taken against those who spread tales of haunting and depreciated the value of property. Centuries ago the writer of *Ecclesiasticus* wrote, 'there are spirits that are created for vengeance and in their fury they lay on grievous torments'. He did not know that these evil spirits were later to be known as poltergeists, the worst and most dangerous forms of haunting. They have the power and tyranny to take over a house day and night in so frightening a way that they have driven the owners out, as in the story of Willington Mill. They made life a hell for the Reverend Samuel Wesley and his family in Epworth Parsonage.

It is a pity that so many ghost stories are associated with graves and graveyards, but this is inevitable, since the whole meaning of the occult is communication between the living and the dead. The word 'ghost' is defined by the *Oxford English Dictionary* as 'the soul of a deceased person spoken of as appearing to the living'. Curiously it also gives two other definitions, for in 1485 a ghost was a good spirit, in 1529 an evil spirit – a strange and swift transition, to say the least. Both Owen Glendower and Hotspur seemed to have been able to deal with spirits in Shakespeare's *Henry IV Part 1*:

> Glendower: I can call spirits from the vasty deep.
> Hotspur: Why; so can I; or so can any man; but will they
>   come when you do call for them?

However, the majority of people prefer not to dabble in the occult.

Many ghost stories deal with gruesome subjects calculated to make the flesh creep and strike fear into the hearts of listeners when told round a blazing fire and by candlelight, as they were before the days of central heating and electric light. The stories in this book have purposely covered a wide range of ghosts, quiet, happy, helpful, warning, rewarding and solicitous ghosts, for they abound in legend and folklore and certainly outnumber the gruesome ones. Surely the two most gentle and kindly ghosts in Britain are the Saxon soldier of Tintern Abbey and 'Dickie' of Tunstead Farm in Derbyshire.

The most remarkable evidence of the existence of ghosts has come in 1987: the monks haunting Magdalen College, Oxford (see p.70) and the reaction of scientists at the Goonhilly Earth Station on the Lizard Downs in Cornwall. The communications station was built in 1965 and the mighty 100-foot diameter 'saucers' track satellites 25,000 miles away. The site chosen was one of Britain's earliest burial grounds where a large colony of Druids lie near one of the 'dishes'. The men who work at the station are often reluctant to service it at night and many of them have heard singing in the silence. It has been reported by one technician to a London daily newspaper:

Many of us have heard voices, strange singing sounds. A few people say they have seen figures moving in and around the dish. We are all technically-minded people here, not prone to believing in ghosts, but not one of us relishes the thought of going out there in the dark, and quite a few have returned rather white around the gills.

There seems little to add, only to quote the learned Dr Samuel Johnson's words, typical and to the point regarding the occult. 'All argument is against it but all belief is for it.'

1 East Anglia

Cambridgeshire: The Happy Ghosts of Sawston Hall

Throughout the four centuries or more during which the Roman Catholic and Royalist family of Huddleston have occupied Sawston Hall, they have lived with ghosts. This haunted, splendid Tudor mansion at Sawston, in Cambridgeshire, came into their possession through an alliance with the powerful house of Nevill.

The Huddlestons, originally a Cumberland family, came south during the Wars of the Roses in the fifteenth century. Sawston Hall was then owned by John Nevill, brother of the Earl of Warwick, 'The Kingmaker'. Isabel, John Nevill's fifth daughter, a young, beautiful and very rich woman, co-heiress of the Duke of Bedford, married Sir William Huddleston. Their grandson, Sir John, rebuilt the house in 1553 after it had been destroyed by fire. The house was burnt down the night 'Bloody' Mary Tudor slept there whilst hiding from her pursuers, the adherents of the cause of Lady Jane Grey backed by the Duke of Northumberland.

Throughout the eventful and chequered history of the family, which more than once threatened their extermination, the ghosts have flitted about the rooms and grounds, the proverbial Grey Lady amongst them. Music and laughter have been heard in empty rooms, door latches have been heard clicking up and down during the night for no apparent reason. Only one of the ghosts is malevolent, the rest are harmonious and harmless.

When a leading psychic expert visited the house some years ago, actually sleeping in the bed 'Bloody' Mary occupied on that fateful night, he found himself disturbed far more than any other visitor. He failed to give any explanation of the mysterious person who kept clicking the door latch up and down, other than defining the ghost as a 'protective' one.

Before the roof of the magnificent Great Hall collapsed a few years ago, the house was open to the public, who could see the tapestries, the oak panels, the historic Tapestry Room containing the bed where the Queen had slept, and the one-hundred-foot Long Gallery. About the time Major Anthony Eyre, nephew of Captain Huddleston, decided to open his house to the public, a new mystery occurred. He was standing in the Great Hall, waiting for the ladies he had engaged as guides to arrive. Suddenly there came echoing down the staircase leading to the top floor the joyous sounds of girlish laughter. As he was all alone in the house, he could not understand who it was. He at once went upstairs and began a thorough search of the rooms, but found no one at all. As the guides were beginning to arrive he had to go downstairs again to meet them, the mystery of that clear laughter unsolved.

The sound of music was first heard in 1930 by Captain Huddleston's wife. She heard a spinet being played in one of the upper rooms. At the time she was standing in the hall at the foot of the stairs and the music was clear and unmistakable. What puzzled her most of all was the fact that the only instrument in the house was an old harpsichord. This was in an empty locked room and had not been played for a very long time. When she told her husband he simply said, 'Nonsense!' He quickly changed his mind, some little time later when a guest asked them both, 'What is that tinkling music I keep on hearing?' After that the sound of a spinet being played upstairs was often heard. Then it ceased and has not been heard since. 'Which is a pity, because it was so lovely,' said Mrs Huddleston. Did the playing and the laughter come from the Long Gallery? Were they expressions of the happiness of members of the family at their freedom from the cruel persecutions of the Catholics under Queen Elizabeth?

The most haunted room in the house is the Tapestry

Room upstairs. At the end of the last century a retired housemaid recounted what she had experienced there. She had always ignored the stories of the other maids who spoke of the three loud warning knocks before the door opened. One day, when she was kneeling down to attend to the fire, she saw 'the grey thing', as she called it, pass right by her. She was so terrified that she ran out of the room into the Little Gallery, falling down the stairs leading into it and hurting herself badly. Curiously enough the Grey Lady, whoever she was, has never been seen since.

Not only is the Tapestry Room haunted but also the adjoining Panelled Bedroom, neither of them having ever been used by the family. When there were many guests both rooms were occupied, though very naturally visitors were never told the rooms were haunted. However, many of them soon discovered the truth and declined to occupy them a second time when invited again to the house.

The ghost of 'Bloody' Mary Tudor has been seen in the Tapestry Room and in the grounds, 'without a shadow of a doubt' according to one housekeeper. Since the Queen's portrait, attributed to Guillim Stretes, hangs in the hall it is reasonable to suppose the housekeeper was right. Indeed, considering the circumstances surrounding the Queen's brief and almost fatal stay in the house, it is surprising that her ghost has not been seen there more often.

On 7 July 1553 a single event almost brought the end of Sawston Hall and the family of Huddleston who gave 'Bloody' Mary shelter there. Just before then, the boy king Edward VI had died of consumption. This left Mary Tudor rightful Queen of England. The powerful and ruthless Duke of Northumberland, however, had another idea. This was to bypass the Tudor line by marrying his son Lord Guildford Dudley to Lady Jane Grey and proclaim her Queen of England. He first seized the Tower of London and its armoury, then posted a double line of armed guards round Greenwich Palace to prevent news of the king's death becoming known. He next sent his other son, Robert, at the head of a cavalry troop, to capture Mary as she reached Hoddesdon on her way to London. Warned of this plot by one of her spies, Mary willingly accepted the offer of Sir John Huddleston to lodge for the night at Sawston Hall. She slept that night in the Tapestry Room, occupying the great four-poster bed which is still to be seen there, the proudest possession of the family.

As dawn broke, one of the guards posted on the roof of the house gave the alarm. A band of cavalry were rapidly approaching the house. Mary was immediately aroused. Sir John suggested his women should be allowed to disguise her as a milkmaid, and thus arrayed she was hustled out of the house into the courtyard, from which she rode pillion behind one of Sir John's grooms, Sir John himself escorted her.

At a short distance from the house, on a hilltop, the little party looked back anxiously to see if they were being pursued. Not only had Northumberland's men surrounded the house, but, thwarted by the escape of Mary they had set fire to it and it was soon blazing fiercely. 'Let it blaze,' said Mary with calm dignity. 'When I am Queen I'll build the Huddlestons a better house.'

Northumberland was defeated and executed. Queen Jane, who had reigned only nine days, was also beheaded. During her reign Queen Mary fulfilled her promise to the Huddleston family, ordering Sawston Hall to be rebuilt with stone brought from the nearby Cambridge Castle. After her marriage to Philip of Spain she honoured Sir John with a knighthood and appointed him a Privy Counsellor, Vice-Chamberlain and Captain of His Majesty's body-guard.

But the Huddlestons paid dearly for that single night of hospitality, for when Elizabeth came to the throne her persecution of the Catholics was almost worse than her sister's had been of the Protestants. Sawston Hall, like all the other loyal Catholic households, had its priest-hole built by Nicholas Owen, the greatest of all Catholic crafts-men of his time. Hidden in the thick walls, its trapdoor was cunningly concealed within the floorboards covering the entrance to it.

From the very beginning of Elizabeth's long reign, Jane Huddleston stubbornly refused to attend the enforced Protestant church services. She was imprisoned and condemned to be 'pressed' to death. This was a particularly savage and slow form of death, at one time meted out to pirates. The victim, shackled hand and foot and unable to move, had one heavy weight upon another placed on his or her stomach until suffocation caused a slow and painful death, prolonged in its agony by lifting a weight and then lowering it again. Fortunately Jane escaped this barbarous torture for her sentence was commuted to life imprisonment, from which she was not released until the death of Elizabeth. John Rigby, her faithful steward, was less fortunate, for he was hanged, drawn and quartered for the same offence. It is all the more surprising, therefore, that his ghost does not move about Sawston Hall.

The leading clairvoyant, Harry Price, who once came there, slept in the very bed in the haunted Tapestry Room which 'Bloody' Mary had occupied. He had a very disturbed night indeed, but was absolutely certain that the spirit was a 'protective' one, anxious for the safety of all who slept both there and in the adjoining Panelled Room. Such a verdict must be of great comfort to the Huddleston family, for throughout their history they have had great need of such protection. The expert added that the spirit might be that of a night-watchman or a guard.

The clairvoyant's decision to sleep the night not only in the haunted room but also in the actual great four-poster bed with its rich hangings which so fortunately escaped the fire on that fatal day, required no little courage. He confidently set his alarm for seven o'clock, greatly puzzled and disturbed when it went off at four o'clock. At the very same moment, he distinctly heard someone moving the bedroom door latch up and down, as if about to enter. At five o'clock the alarm went off again, and once more he heard the sound of the latch being lifted. At that moment he clearly heard someone moving about in the empty and locked Panelled Bedroom behind the Tapestry Room. The

alarm went off again at six o'clock and finally at the set time
of seven o'clock, each time accompanied by the rattling of
the door latch.

Just before this event, and unknown to the clairvoyant, a
similar disturbance had been experienced by a young un-
dergraduate. As the house was full at the time of his visit he
had been put in the Tapestry Room without being told it
was haunted. He had gone to bed with a heavy cold, but
suitably dosed for it. In the morning, when he came down
to breakfast, he surprised his hostess by thanking her for
looking in on him during the night. His hostess assured
him she had done no such thing. 'Oh, but I know you did,'
he answered, then told her how he had been awakened by
somebody's footsteps outside his room, followed by three
loud, clear knocks on the door. Believing it to be his
hostess, he had cried out: 'Come in!', but no one entered
the room. There was an uneasy silence, then the latch was
rattled again. Once more he called 'Come in!' but still no
one entered, and there was the same uneasy silence. By
now he was thoroughly frightened, and he spent the rest of
the night with his head buried under the clothes, waiting
anxiously for daylight and the moment when he could get
up and go downstairs.

Shortly after these incidents Father Martindale, a well-
known priest, came to stay at Sawston Hall and was put in
the Panelled Bedroom. He too said at breakfast the next
morning that he had had a terribly disturbed night. 'Somebody kept on fiddling with the door latch, but no one came
in,' he said. He was quite positive it was a ghost and was
not anxious to sleep in the room again.

The strangest part of all these stories is that it was the
Grey Lady who was supposed to haunt the room. It does
not seem likely that 'the grey thing' which so terrified the
housekeeper was in any way protective. So who was the
protective spirit? Could it perhaps be the spirit of one of the
guards appointed to watch over Mary that night when she
slept there? This seems as reasonable a theory as any other.

Yet there was one very unpleasant ghost in the house. In
about the year 1800, another Jane Huddleston wrote a letter

to her nephew Richard, at that time in command of the Cambridgeshire Regiment. In it she minutely described something she had heard about the wife of the village tanner. This woman, when entering one of the upstairs rooms at Sawston Hall – Jane does not say which one – was suddenly seized by unseen hands which ripped off almost all her clothes, leaving her ashamed, shocked, and speechless with terror. Though vigorous searches were made throughout the whole house no clue was ever discovered of what must have been a particularly ferocious poltergeist. Years later another woman was similarly attacked, both these acts of violence being totally unaccountable to a family already familiar with a variety of ghosts.

Norfolk: *The Brown Lady: Raynham Hall and Houghton Hall*

The sad ghost known to all who have seen her as the Brown Lady, and supposed to be that of Dorothy Walpole, has never ceased to haunt the splendid seventeenth-century Raynham Hall, Norfolk, the home of the Marquis of Townshend. Though she sometimes appears in the corridors, it is the main staircase that she seems to frequent most. She has been sketched, photographed by reliable Court photographers, and even shot at by a guest. Her first recorded appearances were between 1835 and 1849, her most recent in 1936.

Dorothy was the sister of Sir Robert Walpole, later created Earl of Orford, who built Houghton Hall not far away, said to be the largest country house in Norfolk, and of immense importance to students of eighteenth-century architecture. This house, too, is haunted by the Brown Lady. Sir Robert was Prime Minister to George I, and widely known as 'every man has his value Walpole'. He was the longest-serving and also the first Prime Minister in English political history, and probably the most corrupt.

When in 1730 he built this elegant four-turreted house, he gave William Kent his first major assignment. It is full of beautiful furniture and fine paintings, and would have possessed even more of the latter had not his eccentric and spendthrift grandson, the third Earl, sold ninety-seven of them to the Tsarina of Russia, thus depleting a collection of pictures considered by experts to have been the finest in England. The third Earl sold them to pay for his eccentricities and to maintain the constant and lavish hospitality he offered to the very dubious assembly of scroungers and unscrupulous people who frequented his house at all times.

When building Houghton Hall, Sir Robert Walpole, as he then was, discovered that the village of Houghton 'did not improve his view'. With an arrogance unequalled by few, even in that age, he had the whole village removed to another spot nearby out of sight. It was the abandoned, original village which inspired Oliver Goldsmith to write his poem *The Deserted Village*.

Horace Walpole, the fourth Earl of Orford, epicure, novelist, and prolific letter-writer, preferred not to live there but in the delightful Strawberry Hill at Twickenham. On one of his visits to Houghton he describes how he went to church and was surprised to find all the men sitting on one side of the nave and the women on the other. As there was some talking, the parson glared at them in disapproval, at which one of the women said, 'Sir, it is not among us'. 'So much the better', snapped the parson, 'it will be the sooner over.'

La Rochefoucauld, the great French philosopher, visited Houghton Hall in 1784 and made a sharp comment on the prevalent English habit of heavy drinking after dinner. 'The sideboard', he wrote, 'is furnished with a number of chamber pots, as it is a common practice to relieve oneself while the rest are drinking.' The ghost of Dorothy Walpole is said to haunt Houghton Hall because as well as being neighbours of the Townshends it was Charles Townshend, the second Viscount, who married her as his second wife. Dorothy's ghost is supposed to have visited the Prince

Regent when he was staying there and sleeping in the State Bedroom; he asked to be moved to another room for the rest of his stay.

The Townshends in the fifteenth century were prominent and wealthy through the Law Courts, for Sir Roger was a Justice of the Common Pleas in 1484, and was lawyer to the famous Paston family, the great letter-writers. Charles, 2nd Viscount Townshend, married Dorothy Walpole, becoming politically and agriculturally noted when he introduced the turnip into England and so became universally known as 'Turnip' Townshend. His grandson George took over command of the Quebec Heights from Wolfe, and was later Lord Lieutenant of Ireland.

Dorothy Walpole was said to have been very charming, but frivolous and extravagant in her tastes, which no doubt lost her the affection of her husband. Almost from the start their marriage was an unhappy one. She was a most loving mother and extremely fond of her children. When, for reasons best known to himself, her husband ordered her to be deprived of the children, she was most deeply hurt, and all the more so because they were put under the influence and care of their paternal grandmother, also living in Raynham Hall who was naturally at all times on the side of Lord Townshend in every family quarrel. It is small wonder, therefore, that Dorothy's ghost haunts the Hall, no doubt searching for her children, from whom she was so cruelly and unjustly separated.

Guests at the house who knew nothing of the ghost constantly asked their host, 'who was the lady in brown seen frequently on the stairs?' Her first dramatic appearance was at a Christmas party given by Lord and Lady Charles Townshend. Amongst the guests were a Colonel and Mrs Loftus. The Colonel was a brother of Lady Charles and a cousin to Lord Charles, being a Townshend on his mother's side.

The tradition of the haunting by a brown lady had been almost forgotten since her appearances had recently been rare, so the subject was not mentioned at all during conversation. One night, however, Colonel Loftus and a gentleman named Hawkins sat up rather late over a game of chess; having finished they went upstairs to bed. As they were bidding each other good-night, Hawkins suddenly said: 'Loftus, who is that standing at your sister's door? How strangely she is dressed'. Colonel Loftus, who was short-sighted, put up his glass, a lorgnette, and followed the movements of the figure as it went on along the corridor and disappeared.

The next night he saw her again. To make quite sure she would not escape him this time, he ran up a staircase which he knew would bring him face to face with her. There, in a full light, stood a stately lady in a brown gown of rich brocade with a kind of coif on her head like a nun. Her features were clearly defined but he was horrified to see that where her eyes should have been there were only dark hollows.

'These were the two appearances he described to me', records Lucia Stone in her book *Rifts in the Veil*. 'He even sketched her afterwards to me just after his return from Raynham'. As might have been expected, the re-opening of the haunting legend gave one guest after another some excuse for leaving or not coming again.

There was living in the neighbourhood, however, the redoubtable Captain Marryat, of *Mr Midshipman Easy* fame, who had himself sailed before the mast, and judging from some of his own experiences was not a little psychic. As he was one of their personal friends, the Townshends told him all about the Brown Lady. At that time Norfolk was swarming with poachers and smugglers, and Marryat said at once that it was probably the latter as they often had a secret way into a house, keeping the occupants away by fears of ghosts and hauntings. He offered to spend three nights in the house, adding, 'I'll damn well dispose of them, my lord, with my pistol'. So without more ado the captain moved in.

He was disgusted when he found that he slept quite soundly the first night, having first put a loaded pistol under his pillow. He had been told by Lord Charles that the ghost was supposed to be that of one of his ancestors and that she wore a brown brocade dress and a coif and wimple. There was, he added, a portrait of her in the very room the captain was sleeping in and which was supposed to be the haunted room, so that he could see for himself what she looked like. Marryat snorted, 'That ingenious disguise will not save her from my pistol when I see her'. As the second night passed without her appearance the captain was even more disgusted, thinking that if there really was a ghost, and he did not believe that for one moment, she had known of his intentions and decided not to visit him.

But on the third night something did happen. He was just undressing for bed when two of Lord Townshend's nephews knocked on his door and asked him if he would come and have a look at a new gun which had arrived that day from a London gunsmith, and was in their room. The captain dressed again and picked up his loaded pistol. 'I'd better bring this,' he laughed, 'in case we meet the Brown Lady'. After examining the gun with much admiration, he said good night to them and went to the door. 'Oh, we'll come with you', they said laughingly, 'just in case you meet the Brown Lady'.

The long passage leading to the captain's room was now in darkness as the lights had been extinguished, but half-way along the corridor they saw a light moving towards them. 'It must be one of the maids going to the nursery,' whispered one of the nephews. But for some reason Marryat was more than intrigued by the light which was now coming nearer and nearer. Suddenly he saw the Brown Lady, just as she was in the portrait in his room, in her brown brocade gown and Elizabethan ruff. He cocked his pistol and was about to cry out, 'Halt!' when she herself stopped, standing full in front of him and holding the lamp above her head.

'Then' – to quote the captain's daughter, Florence, who wrote down what her father told her – 'she grinned at me in a most diabolical manner'. At that moment the captain fired full into her face. In a flash the light went out and the Brown Lady vanished. Later a bullet was found embedded in the outer door of the room behind where she had stood.

If Marryat had had any doubts at all of the ghost, the two nephews had not, for all three had seen her as clearly as if she had been a live person. Nor did Lord Townshend disbelieve what they told him; it only confirmed once more the existence of the Brown Lady.

However, in order to trace any trickery, if such there were, Lord Charles Townshend had all the locks and bolts changed throughout the whole house. When the Brown Lady continued to appear he engaged some of the London police force to come to Raynham Hall. To ensure still further security, he required them to wear his household livery. In the event, they discovered nothing at all during their stay and returned to London without seeing the Brown Lady at all.

Another proof positive of her existence came as late as 1936 in a photograph taken by two highly reputable Court photographers who had been sent down by *Country Life* to photograph the rooms for an article on Raynham Hall. Neither Captain Provand nor his assistant, Mr Indra Shira, knew anything at all about the Brown Lady, nor were they psychic in any way, which makes their story as authentic as any about this mysterious ghost. Captain Provand, an art director, had been a professional photographer for over thirty years.

It was 19 September and they made an early start at eight o'clock. After working hard all day they were ready at four o'clock to photograph the great staircase. Provand prepared to take the first picture whilst Shira held the flashlight pistol and stood behind him. As the captain had his head under the black cloth he could not see what Shira suddenly saw. To his amazement Shira watched what he later described as 'an ethereal veiled form moving down the staircase'. He shouted excitedly to the captain, 'Quick! Quick! Are you ready? There's something'.

'Yes,' answered the other from under the cloth. Shira flashed the light and simultaneously the captain took the photograph. When he uncovered his head he asked what all the excitement was about. Shira then told him about the transparent figure he had seen coming down the stairs, saying that he had actually seen the stairs through the figure. The captain laughed heartily for by now there was nobody on the stairs to support his colleague's statement.

They discussed the phenomenon quite freely all the way back to London. The captain was emphatic that only a medium at a séance could take a spirit photograph, or so he had been told. Shira was equally emphatic about the form he had seen, so they had a bet of £5 on the result, as this would show up on the negative if it were true.

They were at work in the darkroom next day when an astonished captain cried out, 'Good Lord, there's something on the staircase after all!' Shira looked at the plate, then they called in a third person from the shop as an extra witness, who saw the negative taken from the developer and put in the hypo. He later said that if he had not himself seen the plate put into the tray of solution he would never have believed it. Both the story and the full-size picture were published in *Country Life* of 26 September 1936. Both partners gave their solemn word of honour that there had been no photographic trickery whatsoever. It was examined by many photographic experts, but no solution could be found for the ghostly figure revealed there.

The photograph clearly shows a figure descending the staircase, a tall woman in flowing white and, as Shira himself saw at the time, the stairs are visible through the form. The face and hands cannot be seen, but the folds of the dress are very clear. From the head hangs a coif or wimple, and below the face a shape which could very easily be that of a ruff.

It is this Elizabethan or Jacobean ruff worn by the Brown Lady which disproves the story of Dorothy Walpole being the ghost, for she lived during the reign of George I when ruffs were very decidedly not worn. So who then is the Brown Lady? Why did she wait until 1835 to make her first appearance? Raynham Hall was built *c*.1630 (probably earlier) when ruffs *were* worn, which seems to indicate she was something to do with the Sir Roger Townshend who built it.

2 The Home Counties

Berkshire: A Miscellany of Ghosts

Berkshire has a wealth of ghost stories, gruesome and otherwise, even humorous, and three ghosts haunt the lovely village of Bucklebury, some eight miles from Newbury. It is hard to think that the neat and tidy churchyard of St Michael's Church was once so haunted than when dark fell over the countryside and midnight struck from the church tower, not a soul would dare venture out from the pretty glebe cottages nearby or the fine old vicarage. Curtains were drawn tightly across the windows of the candle-lit rooms where villagers became nervous at what might happen to disturb their sleep. For some time whisperings and movements had been heard in the churchyard after midnight, strange and unfamiliar sounds and worse still, those who had dared to peep from their curtains or shutters had watched in terror ghostly white figures moving about. Things came to a head when one night, a villager, having dared to peep, gave hair-raising stories of what looked like a funeral procession or something similar.

His story, exaggerated in the passing from mouth to mouth, heightened fear still more, until one tough young farm labourer, goaded on by his fellow workers, was dared to investigate and find out what was going on. After several blank nights his courage, for that it certainly was, was rewarded. Hidden behind a tree with a heavy cudgel near at hand, he saw with bated breath as the last chime of midnight struck four white figures carrying what looked like a corpse on a stretcher. He sprang from his hiding-place with a great yell, waving his cudgel as the figures dropped the stretcher and ran. The corpse lay on the grass wrapped in its white sheet. With even more courage the lad pulled aside the sheet, revealing a large dead sheep stolen from the fields surrounding the church.

Humorous as this story is, it must be remembered that this was the age of body-snatching from graveyards for disposal to hospitals for money and this incident may well have been the reason for the vicar erecting a sentry-box in the churchyard where a guard could keep watch at night against grave-robbers.

A more fearsome ghost was that of the unhappy, wretched Lady Bolingbroke, the beautiful daughter of Sir Henry Winchcombe, descended from Jack of Newbury, the famous clothier. When Lord Bolingbroke, Secretary of State to Queen Anne, fled to France during the reign of George I, stripped of his titles and attainted, he abandoned his wife for another woman. From that moment Lady Bolingbroke really ceased to live, as although he had been unfaithful to her many times and led a very dissipated life, she had been entirely devoted to him. It is said she died of a broken heart, which is not surprising, and her ghost, weeping and clasping her hands together, has often been seen by the fishponds of her beautiful manor house. She has also been seen in the passage leading from the cellars, an escape route used by her husband when he fled to France. More frightening still to those who often saw it was her coach, drawn by six black horses, on the leading one of which sat a headless postillion. Inside the coach sat Lady Bolingbroke dressed all in white.

The third haunting in this village and the surrounding Kennet River countryside happened long before these two. The ghost was an unidentified monster, dreaded by all who saw it and said to 'act very unpleasant'. Unable any longer to stand the ravages of this gross monster the villagers banded together and at last succeeded in killing a mammoth, not a 'ghost', burying it in the river bank. Countless years later it was dug up by accident and a Bucklebury villager managed to identify what could have once been the bladebone of the 'ghost'. He told his story to the local innkeeper, who decided to rename his pub *The Bladebone*, which it still is!

A really gruesome story is that of John Head of West Ilsley who, refusing the demands of the Duke of Cumberland, the 'butcher' of Culloden, to hand over to him his fine stables, found them burned to the ground. The next day he mysteriously disappeared. Many years later his headless body was discovered in his own grounds; later still, when the church was being restored, his head was found. On dark winter nights, four men in black have often been seen carrying a coffin containing John Head's corpse. Even in broad daylight a village woman taking her dog for a walk saw the ghosts and her dog bared its teeth, his hackles up, growling threateningly.

Chieveley has a ghost, the daughter of Philip Weston, a Royalist officer during the Civil Wars. She had fallen in love with one of the enemy, a Roundhead officer. Both he and her father were to take part in a battle the next day and in an effort to solve the problem her father agreed to send her news by trumpet. One blast would announce his own death, two that of her lover, three if both had died. When, after many anxious hours, the girl heard the three dreaded blasts, she rushed out and hurled herself down a very deep well, round which her unhappy and weeping ghost wanders at night. Another ghost of the Civil Wars is that of the sentry who guarded Biggs Cottage on Wash Common, where Essex slept the night before the Battle of Newbury.

The most harmless ghost is probably that of 'Old Tanner' in his knee breeches, wandering aimlessly about Hampstead Norreys churchyard.

The ghost of 'Ungodly Harry' haunts Longworth. He was Sir Harry Marten, MP for Berkshire, whose signature was on the death warrant of Charles I. He was a heavy drinker, a great gambler, fond of dancing-girls and the good life. His ghost is forever searching for something, probably the wine left in his cellars, or the dancing-girls.

One of the more eccentric ghosts in Berkshire, perhaps, is that of 'Old Nobes' of Basildon. He was a wheelwright, owning several cottages and some twenty acres of land, who, during his lifetime, supervised the erection of a dome-shaped cell like a large beehive, where he was finally to be interred, for the simple reason that he was a Dissenter from the church, leaving instructions in his Will 'to be buried in his own ground.' This was his expression of protest against the then prevalent bigotry and persecution. His tomb was of stone, the interior of the roof lined with lead. There was a narrow aperture through which the key that locked the door after his burial was to be thrown inside and the aperture sealed. That tomb may be seen today incised with the words *Nobes's Tomb 1699*.

Though himself religious he was regarded by all in the neighbourhood as an infidel. In spite of the carefully-calculated impregnability of his tomb he had not been dead for long before thieves found a way of opening it and stealing all the lead, which was, and still is, of great value. It was then that his ghost started to haunt the countryside as he rode round his twenty acres of property mounted on a white horse. 'There goes old Nobes on his white horse' became a general joke amongst the many people who saw him often on his tours perhaps looking for the lead-robbers. Indeed the author has recently personally met an old villager, a lady who takes her dog out for a walk in the evenings, who told me with truthful sincerity that she often met 'Old Nobes', who greeted her by taking off his hat and bidding her good evening. She said it never frightened her, but made the dog growl and bark at him until he rode away.

Buckinghamshire: The Haunted Room at Creslow Manor

It was over a hundred years ago, in the year 1850, that the High Sheriff of Buckinghamshire set out on horseback to join a dinner party to which he had been invited at Creslow Manor House in the village of Creslow, down a lane from the Aylesbury to Buckingham road. This fine stone-built house was built in the fourteenth century on the site of an earlier Norman castle. The manor and all its lands belonged to the powerful and rich Knights Hospitaller of St John of Jerusalem and was surrounded by vast areas of pasture land known as Christ's Low, hence Creslow. One field alone covered over 320 acres, where fat cattle grazed for the royal table. In the cellars of the Manor House was the crypt, now all desecrated to stables. These formed part of the oldest farm in Buckinghamshire and its own tiny parish near Whitchurch, 11 miles from the county capital town of Buckingham. The Manor House is one of the oldest existing specimens of its kind in England, and considerable parts of its original structure still remain visible.

The Sheriff had gone about halfway when black clouds began to gather in the sky. He at once hastened his pace in order to avoid a downpour of rain, which now began with a few heavy drops as the thunder and lightning started. He had just managed to reach the door of the house when the storm broke in all its fury. After handing over his horse to be fed and stabled he was met by his host who at once insisted on him staying the night. Though that had not been the Sheriff's original intention, it now seemed advisable to stay and return the following morning. His host apologized that the only room available was said to be haunted.

'Haunted by what?' asked the Sheriff amusedly.

'By an old lady in a rustling silk dress,' answered his host. 'She is seldom seen but has been heard many times by those who sleep in the haunted room, as it has always been called. It may have been hers at one time. She seems to come from the door at the top of the nearest staircase to the room. I am told she has a long silk train and moves with short quick steps. I have never myself seen or heard her though, of course, I would never sleep in the room. Those who have say the rustling is violent as if she were struggling with someone or something. She is said to come up from the old crypt of the former chapel.'

To his surprise, the Sheriff was actually laughing when he had finished his story, answering his host that so far from being perturbed he was rather intrigued. He accepted the fact that ghosts existed, and whilst he had never personally become involved with one, this might be a splendid opportunity for him to find out just how he, a sceptic, would be affected by meeting one. He therefore said he would not return home that night but would occupy the haunted room.

From a physical point of view he knew himself to be more than capable of dealing with ghosts. He was fit, strong, spent most of his time in the open air, and had a clear and reasoning mind. For him it was no problem at all and he at once followed his host upstairs to see the room he was to occupy, where he was left until a manservant was sent up to see to his needs.

'Splendid,' said the Sheriff laughing, 'I will have time to make a preliminary investigation and prepare for a visitation from the other world.'

By now the storm was fierce; the lightning forked and flickered through the heavy clouds as the thunder crashed above the house and the rain roared down. If ever there were a correct atmosphere for a ghost, thought the Sheriff, it was now, and he began to look forward to an encounter with one. Just as he began to investigate, however, the manservant knocked on the door, and entered with a can of hot water, candles and matches. He began to unpack the Sheriff's case and lay out his clothes.

When the High Sheriff went downstairs to join the other guests round the dinner table, there was much laughter and joking as they teased him about the haunted room. None of them had the remotest idea what caused the haunting, but all knew the story of the lady in the silk dress. Nevertheless, the host did not join in the banter. He found it easier for his mental welfare to avoid using the room at all.

Everyone in the room was fully aware of the Sheriff's powerful build, confidence, self-assurance and quiet strength, all of which qualities they felt would be adequate for dealing with any intruder, be they practical joker or even the ghost if indeed there was one. In spite of the most earnest request from his host, the Sheriff positively refused to have either a fire lighted or a night-light provided.

However, to continue his joking, he asked his host for a cutlass and a brace of pistols. With mock solemnity he bade all his fellow guests good-night, trusting and hoping they would be able to sleep as well as he knew he would. He then went upstairs to bed in the haunted room.

By the light of his candle he made a most thorough search of every part of the room, tapping the walls, the panelling and the floorboards, before locking and firmly bolting both doors of the room. Being quite satisfied with his investigations, he undressed and got into bed. The storm had lost its full fury and was passing away, though the continuing heavy rain would have prevented him returning home that night in any case. Glad that he had a comfortable bed, he fell asleep almost immediately, just as he had jestingly told the other guests that he would.

The day dawned with great beauty, a clear and cloudless sky gave no sign at all of the previous night's havoc. One by one the guests came down and assembled in the breakfast-room until, at a sign from their host, they sat down to the breakfast table. There was one empty place. The host's instant expression of alarm was immediately shown in the faces of everyone there. A servant was summoned and ordered to go and wake the High Sheriff in case he had not heard the gong and was still asleep. The servant, as well aware as the others of the haunted room, returned after a few moments, his face pale and anxious. He said he had knocked on the door repeatedly and loudly, but there was no answer. He also said that a jug of hot water he had left outside the door earlier was still there and had not been emptied.

At once, two or three men and the host left the table and ran upstairs. After banging again and again on the door, receiving no response at all, they forced it open and went in. The room was empty. The servants were all questioned. They had neither seen nor heard him since they themselves had got up very early that morning. As the Sheriff was a county magistrate, the host thought he might have gone off early to attend some meeting, or sit on the bench, and had been reluctant to inform or disturb anyone – though this did not seem very feasible and was certainly impolite.

The men went to the stable to see if his horse had gone. It was quietly feeding there. They returned to the now non-plussed and silent breakfast table. Scarcely had they sat down again, when the door opened and the Sheriff walked in. His jocular boisterousness of the night before had completely gone. He was pale, spoke little, and was quite visibly disturbed. It was some considerable time before, in answer to questions, he gave a full account of his experiences of the previous night to the mystified guests.

He explained the thorough investigation of the room he had made, the bolting of the doors, the extinguishing of the candle when he was in bed, and how he had gone to sleep as soon as his head was on the pillow, reckoning not to wake until six o'clock, his customary time of waking and rising. He was suddenly awakened by a sound not unlike that of footsteps, but soft, quick, light, as if of a lady in slippers. By now fully awake, he noticed that the sound was accompanied by the rustling of a heavy silken gown, just as his host had told him the night before. He sprang out of bed and lit the candle, but there was nothing to be seen except his own shadow and the wavering candle flame on the wall. Once again he searched the room very thoroughly. He looked under the bed, up the chimney, in every corner, checked and re-checked the locked and bolted doors; all was as before. There was nothing. Once more he got into bed, admittedly very disturbed and mystified. He noticed it was a few minutes after midnight. Blowing out the candle, he once more fell asleep.

Again he was awakened, this time by a much heavier sound 'like the violent rustling of a stiff silk dress' as he described it. Jumping out of bed in the darkness he leapt at once to the spot where he had heard the sounds. Stretching out both his arms he felt something unmistakably there, but when he encircled what he thought must be a figure his arms met together touching nothing at all. He was now really frightened, and groping for the matches to light the candle again but could not find them. He heard the sounds move to another part of the room. He followed, still in the dark, groping his way along, stooping towards the floorboards trying to prevent the thing from passing under his arms. Then the sound suddenly ceased at a spot beyond his reach. Feeling his way back to the matches, he succeeded in lighting the candle. The room was empty. Remembering exactly where the spot was before the sounds ceased, he made a careful examination there, at the door leading to the crypt. However, there was no sign of anything at all. The Sheriff, perplexed and now fully disturbed by the atmosphere created was finally convinced he had encountered the legendary ghost of Creslow Manor House.

He lay there, leaving his candle burning, waiting anxiously for dawn to break so that he could leave a room he never wanted to see again. It was a changed magistrate who bade his host goodbye after breakfast; no longer the man who had mocked at the whole idea and even welcomed the chance of seeing a ghost.

But who was the lady who found her way from the crypt below the chapel? After all, the Knights Hospitaller did belong to a monastic order where women were not admitted. And why did she visit only that one room and then to a man who had all his life scoffed and jeered at the occult and supernatural? It was almost a challenge from the other world. And why has she never been seen since?

London: *A Ghost from the Sea: Eaton Place*

One of the most astonishing London ghost stories, and there are many, is that of Sir George Tryon. On the night of 22 June 1893, Lady Tryon was holding one of her exclusive 'At Home' parties for carefully selected guests, at her beautiful, very elegant house in Eaton Place, Belgravia. The fashionably-dressed ladies and the gentlemen were chatting together as they sipped their champagne, when suddenly, without any warning, the fine figure of Admiral Sir

George Tryon, in full naval uniform, entered the drawing-room. A great hush fell over the room as he strode across, passing his wife without even acknowledging her, and vanished.

The silence in the room could be heard. Only Lady Tryon, a few of her closest friends and one or two guests knew that Vice-Admiral Sir George Tryon, KCB, was in command of the Mediterranean Squadron then manoeuvring off the coast of Syria. Not one of the people in that room could have guessed that at the very moment he had entered the drawing-room in complete silence, his dead body was lying in the wreckage of his flagship VICTORIA at the bottom of the Mediterranean. If, in that stunned silence, the sight of the Admiral was extraordinary, the reason for his death was even more of a mystery.

His flagship was at the head of one of the two columns steaming along, the other was headed by HMS CAMPERDOWN under the command of Admiral Markham. Admiral Tryon had given specific orders for the two columns to steam parallel with each other until they reached a certain point when they were to turn in towards each other. It was immediately evident to every officer in both columns that such a signal could only end in disaster, but orders from the flagship were not to be challenged and the two columns moved together at the given signal. At some point, one of the officers, perhaps even Admiral Markham, signalled the flagship that in his judgement the distance between the two lines was totally insufficient to avoid a catastrophe, but Sir George was adamant and repeated his original decision.

The battleships, reaching the point given to them, began to turn inwards and there occurred the catastrophe that had been feared, for HMS CAMPERDOWN crashed into the flagship, causing it to heel over and sink with an enormous loss of life. All the engine-room crew were trapped like rats, unable to stop the thrashing screws which cut to pieces the floating bodies of those who had managed to jump overboard. The wrecked and shattered ship sank to the bottom of the sea with Sir George Tryon still on board. With him was one of his midshipmen who had refused the Admiral's last order to save himself and so died with his Admiral. When the sea poured into the fires on board, the two columns of ships and hundreds of men heard a colossal explosion, as the disintegrated flagship vanished from sight. One of the lucky ones to escape this terrible disaster was a young sailor named John Rushworth Jellicoe, who was later to be raised to the Peerage as Earl Jellicoe, Admiral of the Fleet in the famous Battle of Jutland in the First World War.

No one will ever know why so distinguished a naval commander as Sir George Tryon signalled such an order as he did, and actually persisted in its being carried out. A full enquiry was undertaken with great thoroughness, but nothing could be achieved for Admiral Tryon alone could have given his reason and he was not there. One very important statement was made by one of those who had been saved. He told the Court that as the ship began to sink, the voice of Sir George was heard to say 'It is all my fault'.

Could it perhaps have been that at the very moment of that terrible disaster Sir George thought of home and although he had no knowledge of what his wife was doing, he might have passed through the rooms to find her? It is the only possible explanation one can offer for his sudden ghostly appearance in that hushed and crowded drawing-room in Eaton Place, where Lady Tryon was entertaining her guests and friends at an 'At Home' party.

London: The Haunted Barracks of St James's

In the year 1804 the Coldstream Guards were quartered in Recruit House, now the new Wellington Barracks near the Guards Chapel, which was so terribly bombed with great

loss of life in the Second World War. On the night of 3
January a Coldstream Guards sentry named George Jones
was posted on duty between the Cockpit Steps and the lake
in St James's Park. What happened in the very early hours
of that morning created such fear and alarm throughout the
barracks that an immediate full enquiry was ordered by the
commanding officer. Strangely enough, a number of men
made declarations on oath, as well as the principal witness,
the sentry George Jones, before the magistrate Sir Richard
Ford in Westminster.

What was most surprising about the ghost of the headless woman, which the terrified sentry saw, was the emer-
gence of other sightings by several soldiers. They had
probably been afraid to tell anyone what they had seen or
heard for fear of being called a liar, or ridiculed. There is a
ring of truth, however, in both the principal statements
which gives the evidence of real ghosts an unusual authenticity. The sworn statement by George Jones ran thus:

I do solemnly declare that when guard at Recruit House on or
about the 3rd inst., about half past one in the morning, I
perceived the figure of a woman without a head rise from the
earth at a distance of about two feet before me. I was so
alarmed at the circumstance that I had not the power to speak
to it, which was my wish. But I distinctly observed that the
figure was dressed in a red striped gown with red spots
between each stripe, and that part of the dress and figure
appeared to me to be enveloped in a cloud. In about the space
of two minutes, whilst my eyes were fixed on the object, it
vanished from my sight. I was perfectly sober and collected at
the time, and being in great trepidation, called to the next
sentinel, who met me half-way, and to whom I communicated
the strange sight I had seen.

His signed statement is dated 15 January 1804.

The haunted area in question was between the Cockpit
Steps and the canal which at that time ran through St
James's Park and Birdcage Walk. Near there was an empty
house, widely believed to be haunted, although when a

clergyman decided to locate the ghost by passing a night all alone in the house, he neither saw nor heard anything at all.

Another story was told by a Coldstream Guards sentry in a sworn and signed statement which, though at variance with that of George Jones in many details, still rings true. This sentry, one Richard Donkin, was on duty behind the Armoury House at about midnight when he heard disturbing noises from the haunted house. His statement goes on:

At the same time I heard a voice cry out 'Bring me a light! Bring me a light!' The last word was uttered in so feeble and changeable a tone of voice that I concluded some person was ill, and consequently offered them my assistance. I could however, obtain no answer to my proposal although I repeated it several times, and as often the voice used the same terms. I endeavoured to see the person who called out but in vain. On a sudden the violent noise was renewed which appeared to me to resemble sashes of windows lifted hastily up and down but that they were moved in quick succession and in different parts of the house, nearly at the same time, so it seems to me impossible that one person could accomplish the whole business. I heard several of my regiment say they have heard similar noises and proceedings, but I have never heard the calls accounted for.

One of the most important factors in this whole case is that no other Guards regiment, for the barracks were occupied in turns by other regiments, reported any trouble at all. The reason why only Coldstream Guards saw the headless figure and heard the noises from the empty house may well have been because some twenty years previously a Coldstream Guards sergeant had murdered his wife, cutting off her head and throwing both parts of the corpse into the nearby canal. This event could not have been suppressed, it must have been known throughout the barracks and even beyond and could easily have frightened any sentry on duty at night.

Many years later a civilian reported seeing a woman running towards the park from the Cockpit Steps, wearing a red-and-white dress. Another driver nearly killed, as he thought, a woman rushing across the road from the Cockpit Steps. Her dress had been white, but blood-splashed and she was headless. The phantom, as it was, disappeared into the fog. Noises have also been heard from a nearby empty house, but only by the soldiers and not by the owners. In spite of the most thorough investigations being carried out during and after the statements made to the Westminster magistrate, nothing has explained the ghosts and probably nothing ever will now.

London: 'Scratching Fanny' of Cock Lane, Smithfield

In 1893, three-hundred-and-twenty coffins were taken out of the crypt of St John's Church, Clerkenwell. One of them was stained with arsenic and significantly it bore no identification plate. Only speculation then and now could believe that it contained the body of 'Scratching Fanny'. During her lifetime she had been the cause of one of the best-known and most notorious of all ghost stories, becoming, as it did, a national sensation.

In the year 1757 a man named William Kent, whose profession then would have been that of a stockbroker today, took rooms in number 33 Cock Lane, which at that time ran between Newgate Street and West Smithfield, long since demolished. Kent's wife had died two years previously and he now set up in Cock Lane with his wife's sister named Fanny. Later she became universally known as 'Scratching Fanny'. The landlord was named Thomas Parsons and was clerk in the nearby church of St Sepulchre. They had not settled in very long before Parsons asked Kent if he could lend him some money, which Kent did quite willingly.

The couple had been there two years when Fanny became seriously ill and Kent was obliged to ask Parsons to repay the money he had loaned him. For some reason known only to himself, Parsons became angry, refused to repay the money and a violent quarrel broke out, which developed into a feud, Parsons becoming more resentful and increasing in animosity towards Kent. During Fanny's continuing illness Kent was obliged to go into the country to attend a wedding-party, where he stayed a few days.

While he was away, Parsons' daughter Elizabeth had shared the same bed as Fanny, presumably to keep her company. Fanny was ill and very alarmed at what was happening. She told Parsons that there had been mysterious, loud noises during the days and nights, tappings and rappings on the walls and she was convinced that these were given by someone or something as a warning of her impending death.

Parsons tried to comfort her, feeling that her illness gave her illusions. Since a cobbler lived and worked in the house next door, he said that the noises came from his hammering and from nowhere else. Fanny was not dissuaded, since she knew the cobbler did not work at night or on a Sunday. Parsons nevertheless decided to invite one or two neighbours into the house to talk to Fanny. They were greatly distressed to find Fanny so ill and even suggested that Fanny's dead sister was causing the disturbances, because Fanny and Kent were cohabiting.

When Kent returned and found out what had been happening, he decided to act, suggesting that he and Fanny should immediately make Wills in each other's favour, to which she agreed and this was carried out. In spite of Elizabeth Parsons being allowed to visit Fanny, her father's resentment of Kent became even more pronounced and he still refused to repay the loan. Kent then did two things. He placed the refusal of Parsons to pay his debt into the hands of his attorney and moved Fanny and himself out of Cock Lane to new lodgings in Bartlet Court, Camberwell, where Fanny could start a fresh life away from all the noises, tappings and raps that had made her so afraid. In spite of this Fanny died only a few months later, in 1760, according to her death certificate of the then prevalent and dreaded disease smallpox. She was buried in St John's Church, Clerkenwell.

There is no record of what happened after Fanny's death, but in 1762 'The Cock Lane Ghost' became a sensation and an enigma, not only for the eighteenth century, but for posterity. The ghost was known as 'Scratching Fanny'. All London was convinced that her spirit had returned and began to control, if that is the word, the body of Elizabeth Parsons, perhaps out of revenge for what her father had done to Kent. She appeared as a figure standing by Elizabeth's bed. Wherever she slept Fanny haunted her, reducing the child to constant shivering and trembling, perspiration and great fear, so that she, too, was sure it was Fanny's ghost. She so convinced her father, that he took every precaution to avoid the ghost from appearing. He even stripped the wainscoting and had all the floorboards pulled up, but all in vain for Fanny continued to appear. In final desperation, Parsons employed a nurse called Mary Frazer to see if she could do anything medically to help his daughter recover.

Mary Frazer was not long in the house and the room where Elizabeth slept, before she confirmed the reports of noises, tappings and raps on the walls of the rooms. Sure that she had found the reason for the mystery she informed Parsons that she was certain about the raps, if not of the other disturbances. The raps, in her opinion, could only be messages requiring answers. This form of code, she told him, could be broken by one rap meaning 'yes' and two raps meaning 'no' to questions asked by someone, and since it was his daughter, he should be the one to ask the questions. Whether Parsons did take notice of what she said, or whether he deliberately made up the results, he swore that all the disturbances in the house were caused by Fanny claiming she had been poisoned by Kent, who had given her a draught of ale which contained red arsenic and that her spirit would not rest until Kent was caught and hanged for murder.

This incredible deduction very soon came to the knowledge of the pamphleteers, waiting like hyenas for any
morsel of gossip, lies, slander or scandal that could be
passed round the taverns and coffee-houses. These were
quickly followed by the printing press owners and the
various versions of stories about 'The Cock Lane Ghost'
poured from the presses. There were stories of Elizabeth
Parsons confined to her bed from which constant 'scratch-
ings' and sounds of raps on wood were heard wherever she
was or went; of a shrouded figure without hands appearing
to Elizabeth as she lay in bed, quivering and trembling
with terror until it vanished. There were added stories of
witnesses who saw luminous apparitions *with* hands
standing by the bed. Headlines in the Press proclaimed
'Scratching Fanny in the House of Wonder'.

Such were the stories gathered by the Press, the ballad-
mongers and the pamphleteers that the sensation spread
right across England and even abroad. At first, people from
nearby came to the house to hear for themselves what was
going on with Elizabeth Parsons and the reputed ghost
who controlled her shakings and knockings. The rumours
even attracted highly intelligent and learned men; writers
such as Daniel Defoe, Oliver Goldsmith (who wrote an
account) and Dr Johnson who was strangely and inordin-
ately interested in ghosts and the supernatural. Even
Horace Walpole came to see, 'wondering if there might be
something in the mystery', as he said.

Dr Johnson, having thoroughly investigated the case
decided to join many others in a visit to St John's Church in
Clerkenwell where the ghost had promised to rap on its
own coffin, but they were rewarded only by complete
silence. Even such notables as the Duke of York, accompanied by Lady Northumberland, Lord Hertford and Lady
Mary Coke condescended to visit the scene and William
Hogarth did a print entitled 'Credulity, Superstition and
Fanaticism' to ridicule the whole Cock Lane story. Lord
Hertford wrote a graphic account of his visit to 'the wretch-
edly small and miserable house in which fifty people were
crowded by the light of one candle about the bed of the

child to whom the ghost comes'.

What had started as a mystery, caused by Fanny's visit from the dead, demanding that her lover Kent should be arrested, tried and hanged, now aroused considerable doubts. First the people, then the papers, turned to a vilification of both Kent and Parsons, then to a belief that the ghost did not exist. More serious was the story that Parsons had administered the arsenic in a draught of hot ale to the deceased Fanny. These latest suspicions finally decided the authorities to make a thorough examination of the whole case, most especially the child Elizabeth Parsons so tormented by 'Scratching Fanny' that her own death appeared imminent.

The carefully selected investigators went at once to 33, Cock Lane and the results of their examination were more sensational than when the first news of 'The Cock Lane Ghost' was reported in the Press. The principal clue to the mystery came when the examiners found that when they held the hands of the child all her trembling and the noises of knocking stopped; but as she squirmed and wriggled to free her hands the knocking sounds and trembling began again. Suddenly they discovered the reason for the knocking. Between her stays, the child had hidden a small wooden board on which she had beaten out the knocks and raps as she quivered and trembled in the bed, watched by the people crowded into the room.

The results were immediate, rapid and sensational. Charges and arrests were made; Mary Frazer, Parsons, his wife and daughter Elizabeth were all indicted by Kent who, far from being 'hanged' was awarded several hundred pounds to be paid to him by all concerned. Parsons was sentenced to be placed three times in the pillory at the corner of Cock Lane, followed by two years imprisonment, his wife for one year and Mary Frazer for six months. 'Scratching Fanny's' ghost never again returned.

There are still unanswered and unsolved points. How was it possible for a young child to deceive many hundreds of people, high intellectuals as well as illiterates, by operating such a crude insertion of a piece of wood in her stays?

How was it that the coffin examined by Dr Samuel Johnson and an assembly of men was identified as Fanny's coffin when later it was recorded that there was no identity plate on it? How was the stain of arsenic not visible at the first sight and visible at the last sight? Whose idea was it in the first place and did Fanny ever really communicate with Elizabeth?

It took the German Luftwaffe to dispose of any evidence there might have been in St John's Church, Clerkenwell when it was reduced to ruins in 1941 during the heavy bombing of London. If 'Scratching Fanny's' coffin had ever been there, no sign of it was left when the crypt was finally cleared of the mess left by the bombs and incendiaries. From the very beginning until the end the story of the Cock Lane Ghost has been an enigma, an insoluble mystery for two-and-a-quarter centuries. It seems likely to remain so.

Surrey: The Infamous Lord Lyttelton of Pit Place

The most remarkable and authenticated story of a death-warning ghost in the history of British occultism is that of the infamous and dissipated Thomas, 6th Baronet and 2nd Lord Lyttelton of Frankley, a most ancient and distinguished family in Worcestershire. When Dr Johnson was told the full story of his death, which was widely circulated in the taverns and coffee-houses of London, he remarked, 'It is one of the most extraordinary stories I have ever heard'.

His lordship had recently returned from Ireland to his Mayfair house in Hill Street suffering from suffocating fits, which were probably caused by his excesses. He had a few friends staying with him, including Lord Fortescue, Lady Flood wife of an Irish politician, the two daughters of Mrs Amphlett (all three of whom he had seduced), and his uncle

Baron Westcote, who kept a detailed authentication of all that went on up to the time of his nephew's death.

On Thursday, 24 November 1779, just before midnight, Lord Lyttelton was suddenly awakened by what he himself described as 'the sound of fluttering wings as if from a dove'. Drawing back the heavy curtains of his great four-poster bed he was confronted by a tall figure dressed in white, pointing a finger threateningly straight at him. Confused and astonished by this apparition it was seconds before he could ask who she was. 'Prepare to die within three days,' the phantom answered and vanished.

'His lordship was much alarmed,' his uncle recorded, 'and called for a servant from a closet adjoining who found him much agitated and in a profuse perspiration. The circumstance had a considerable effect all the next day on his spirits.' When he came down to breakfast his lordship was very quiet and looked badly shaken, even more so when, being pressed for a reason for his gravity, he told his friends all that had happened, which brought a stunned silence from them all. He then said that he had a busy day ahead of him in the House of Lords opposing an important Bill and that it was going to be a very difficult day indeed after the night before.

Lord Lyttelton, who was elegant, handsome, rich and had never in his short life been a credit to his family, was born on 30 January 1744 and educated at Eton and Oxford. It was at the latter that he began an affair with the daughter of the distinguished General Warburton, the first of many illicit affairs. It created such a scandal that he was forced to go abroad under the pretence of making the Grand Tour customarily made in those times by wealthy aristocrats. When the gossip had died down, he returned and after his father's death inherited the title.

He was soon once more involved with women and wine, riotous parties with notorious cronies in his house in Mayfair and his country residence in Surrey, details of which circulated both in London and Epsom. In an effort to reform he married Apphia, widow of Joseph Peace, Governor of Calcutta. At the same time, he was conducting another affair with a barmaid named Sarah Harriss, which the disgusted editor of the *Morning Post* exposed, once more forcing his lordship to hide abroad.

He was no sooner back than he had an affair with a Mrs Amphlett whom he seduced as well as her two daughters, the shock of which caused the death of the mother from a broken heart but did nothing to stop him continuing with the daughters with whom he was constantly seen and who now lived in his Mayfair house as guests.

The Friday passed normally and he returned from Westminster in good health and seemingly free of worry about his dream. But the next morning when he came down to breakfast and saw his guests looking anxious and silent he asked, 'Are you all thinking of the ghost? I am as well as ever I was in my life. You are foolish and fearful.' Later during the day, he told them all he had decided they should go to his Surrey residence and instructed them to pack their things and to set off as soon as they were ready.

His Surrey house was a large gloomy villa called Pit Place because it was built on the site of an old chalk-pit near Epsom. It was built of stone from Nonsuch, an old royal palace, with a great gateway, over which stood two stone lions. It was in Church Street and quite near the church, the street itself continuing up to the Downs and the modern buildings of Epsom College today. He was in good form, even joking about 'bilking the ghost', boasting that he was still alive on the second day of the warning and saw no reason why there should not be a third.

He came down to breakfast the next morning quite unperturbed as he had slept well. 'If I live over tonight', he joked, 'I shall have jockeyed the ghost for this is the third day'. The day passed pleasantly enough in spite of the fact that he had another of his attacks. He sat down to dinner at the customary time of five o'clock and ate well, though one of the guests noticed when he was taking his soup 'he had a rising in the throat'. For supper he ate an egg and then went up to bed in the Oaken Chamber. It was eleven o'clock. 'But', said another witness, 'he only thought it was eleven o'clock, having put on the clock to deceive himself and the

ghost.' A story much later given out was that unbeknown
to Lyttelton his guests had put *all* the clocks on, in order to
deceive him and give him comfort, so that he really retired
at ten o'clock.

When he was in his bed the servant, Stuckey, appeared
with the prescribed dose of rhubarb and mint-water, presumably a remedy for his increasing fits. As the servant
stood there Lyttelton noticed he was stirring the mixture
with a toothpick, and calling him 'a slovenly dog' he
ordered him to fetch a teaspoon at once. 'On the man's
return', it was reported by one who collected all the statements later, 'he found his master in a fit, and the pillow
being placed high, his chin bore hard upon his neck. The
servant, instead of relieving his lordship on the instant
from his perilous situation, ran, in his fright, and called for
help; but on his return he found his lordship dead.' It was
27 November 1779 and he was only thirty-five years old. As
he had no issue the Peerage expired.

Lord Lyttelton had a close friend named Andrews whose
part in the epilogue to this whole drama is even more
remarkable. Andrews later wrote:

> It is true that he himself thought he was to die at a given hour,
> and the clock was put on in order to deceive him into comfort.
> It is also true that he was found dead with his watch in his
> hand, at but a few minutes after the time he mentioned would
> be his last . . . The coincidence of events with prophecy was
> at any rate the most remarkable.

Miles Peter Andrews, MP for Bewdley, was a lifelong
crony of Lyttelton, and had previously invited him to join a
weekend party at his house in Dartford, Kent, but Lyttelton, either because he forgot to let him know, or because of
his own anxiety, failed to turn up. In either case he did not
let Andrews know of his intentions. As it turned out,
Andrews himself was feeling so unwell that he left his
guests to entertain themselves and went off to bed. He had
fallen asleep but was suddenly awakened by the curtains of
his four-poster bed being pulled aside, and there standing

before him was Lord Lyttelton, in his nightcap and wearing the flower-figured bedgown Andrews kept there for his friend's frequent visits.

Half asleep as he was he thought Lyttelton had after all turned up, though late, and hearing Andrews was not well had come up to say good-night to him; but the figure made no move. Andrews, however, knew better than all his friends Lyttelton's partiality for practical jokes, not always free of cruelty. Believing now that this was another trick he cried out irritably, 'So you're up to one of your jokes. Go to bed or I'll throw something at you'. As the figure still did not move Andrews, now quite angry, picked up one of his slippers from the floor, then paused as the figure spoke for the first time.

'It's all over with me, Andrews,' it said mournfully, and at that Andrews hurled the slipper at the figure as it retreated to the door of the adjoining closet. Andrews, suddenly feeling something strange was happening, jumped out of bed and followed it, but as it reached the door it vanished. Opening the closet door Andrews saw that it was empty, the door on the other side was locked and bolted, and there, on the peg behind the door was the flower-figured bedgown Lyttelton had been wearing. It was eleven o'clock.

None of the servants summoned by the now frightened Andrews had seen or heard Lyttelton. They were immediately ordered to refuse him admittance if he did come. Yet, though scared, Andrews still believed it might be a joke after all, and went back to bed. The next morning he was informed of his friend's death at Epsom at eleven o'clock the previous night. Hearing the news he fainted 'and was not his own man again for three years.'

The whole story of Lord Lyttelton's death did not at once come out, though rumours were rife, and it became embellished as details were added by all who knew him, principally by his guests. What did seem certain to them all, however, and was very readily accepted, was the belief that the white lady who appeared with her warning of death to the man who had seduced not only her but her daughters as well, was Margaret Amphlett. In his Will he had left her £5,000, perhaps in repentance.

For many years after Lord Lyttelton's death, people visited the Oaken Chamber where the warning had been fulfilled in spite of the fact that the clock had been put back to delude both the lord and the ghost. But from that day to this, the mystery of Lyttelton's ghost appearing to Andrews at the very minute of eleven o'clock has never been solved, nor, for that matter, that eleven o'clock was the time appointed, for it was not Mrs Amphlett's ghost which had given a time. She had said, 'Prepare to die within three days.'

3 The Heart of England

Cheshire: A Ghostly Funeral Procession at Lyme Park

The large and splendid stone house of Lyme, built in the sixteenth and eighteenth centuries, is near Disley. Various members of the ancient and distinguished Legh family have added rooms and extensions throughout the centuries. Of the original Tudor house only the gateway with its strange ornament, built by Sir Piers Legh, is still standing; its tower was removed in 1725 and set up as a folly in the huge deer-park surrounding the house.

In that same year the Italian architect, Giacomo Leoni was called in to modernize the whole building. He set about this in great style, adding an impressive west front facing the lake and not unnaturally making the whole building resemble an Italian palace. The house and park are haunted by one of the rarest of all phantoms, the funeral procession of Sir Piers (or Percy or Peter) Legh.

I am indebted to Mr Bamford, Chester Librarian, for sending me two extracts from the Ballad of Sir Percy Legh which, he informs me, is the earliest printed version of the story he can trace. The three turgid and not very poetic stanzas here quoted are a part of some fifty stanzas, being the most relevant to the hauntings referred to in the introduction. It goes as follows:

Ballad of Sir Percy Legh

In the park at Lyme, near the Hall, is a beautiful conical hill crowned with trees, which has been called from time immemorial "The Knight's Low", and is supposed to have been the burial-place of one of the earlier knights of the family so long resident there. In another part of the estate, adjoining a stream which runs through the park, is a field which has always been known within record as "The Lady's Grave," and also as "The Field of the White Lady." The ballad is founded on a tradition related to the author when on a visit at Lyme by the late Mr Legh. It is said, that at midnight "a muffled sound, as of a distant funeral peal, is often borne on the wind, and that at this time a shadowy procession of mourners may be seen wending towards the Knight's Low, bearing a coffin and pall, and followed by a lady arrayed in white, and apparently in deep distress." The adjuncts to this scene were suggested by Mrs Legh.

The main incidents of the ballad are founded on fact. Sir Piers, or Percy Legh of Lyme, Knight Banneret, following his grandfather's example, engaged in his sovereign's continental warfare, and dying at Paris of honourable wounds received on the field of Agincourt, was brought over to England to be interred.

> HARK! what means that sound
> That low and murmuring swell,
> That dies away and comes again
> As 'twere a distant funeral knell.
>
> Hark again! that wail
> Borne on the passing gale,
> Breaking from the neighb'ring height
> The solemn stillness of the night.
>
> And see the red deer clustering round,
> Intently listen to the sound,
> And peer into the vacant space,
> As though some strange sight met their gaze.

A few confusing points in the Ballad are at variance with historical facts, as so often happens in legends handed down orally. Indeed the whole original tradition was told to the author of the Ballad by Thomas Legh who died at the age of sixty-four in 1857, so that the legend must have been current long before 1857. It could easily have been orally distorted by domestic servants, or even the owners them-selves over the centuries, before John Leigh put it together and had his Ballad published in Manchester by Edwin Slater in 1861. Further confusion is caused by the various spellings of the family Christian names and surnames.

Mr Bamford points out that Sir Piers was *not* buried in the Knight's Low but in Macclesfield church. He does not know where the name of Blanche (mentioned in the Ballad) comes from, but it would be suitable for a white lady, and Sir Piers did have a daughter named Blanche. The historical facts are that Sir Piers married Joan, daughter of Sir Gilbert de Haydock, and was buried in Macclesfield church where his father lay. Sir Piers was wounded at the Battle of Agin-court, fighting as a Knight Banneret under Henry V, dying in Paris on 18 June 1422, after which his body was brought to England. It is not improbable that he was laid in the Knight's Low before being taken to Macclesfield. His father was beheaded during the bitter struggle between John of Gaunt, Duke of Lancaster and King Richard II.

The main mystery about the haunting is the phantom funeral procession, which quite inexplicably has no horse-drawn hearse; even more mysterious is the White Lady who was apparently not the wife of Sir Piers, according to one version, but a lady who loved him and died of grief when news was brought to her of his death. The Lady's Grave in the Ballad was in a meadow of that name near the River Bollin where her corpse was found.

As if this haunting were not enough there is yet another, not in the grounds, but within the house itself. The facts concerning this one are equally vague and unauthenti-cated. There are very many beautiful rooms in the house and one of these has been called the 'Mary Queen of Scots Room' and also 'The Ghost Room'. She certainly stayed there, for a reliquary which belonged to her is there, but whether she haunts the room called after her is another matter. The fact that she was imprisoned in Lyme for a while may have made her haunt the house.

Her room was supposed to have been connected by a secret passage leading to a building in the Park called Lyme Cage. The house and her room is supposed to be haunted by the sound of distant bells ringing at night, but there is no evidence that her ghost has ever been seen. In the room she once occupied, presumably closely watched over by her gaolers, there is a secret chamber and this is the one presumably known as 'The Ghost Room'. Many years ago, though no exact date is recorded, the skeleton of a priest was discovered. He had starved to death in what could have been some kind of priest's hole, used by them to hide in if there was the slightest threat of danger. It would be very easy to imagine that the deeply religious Mary Queen of Scots could have had a priest smuggled in, who died after her departure from Lyme. Yet even if one assumed all this, there is no evidence of the priest's ghost anywhere in the house. The late Christina Hole, whose knowledge of ghost-lore is unsurpassed and whose accuracy is indisputable, categorically states that 'No wandering spirit has been seen'. Since this has never been challenged or disputed it is simpler to accept it, as one must do with so many ghost stories.

Chesire: *Thurleston Old Hall*

In the history of ghosts surely the most curious tale is the one told to Lord Halifax by his artist friend Reginald Easton, who actually drew a ghost and swore to his dying day the authenticity of his story. Lord Halifax was so deeply impressed by his friend's story that he actually wrote it all down and later published it in 1936 in the strangest of all ghost books, *Lord Halifax's Ghost Book*.

The family concerned named Cobb were tenants at Thurleston Old Hall in Cheshire, and having been told by friends of an artist named Reginald Easton Mr Cobb wrote asking him to visit him in order to make miniature paintings of the children. Easton was pleased to accept the task and set out on the journey. He was very surprised to find the house full of guests when he arrived, but Mr Cobb told him not to worry as they had a room for him. Easton found the children very beautiful and arranged to paint them the next morning. He also found his host and hostess to be a charming couple. The only problem seemed to be about the room where he was to sleep, as a sudden muttering and whispered conversation became apparent between Mr and Mrs Cobb he caught the words 'It can't be helped, there is no other.' The words puzzled Mr Easton although he thought the room might be draughty or too small or even damp, and he rather embarrassed his host by asking him if the room was all right or if he was inconveniencing them when they had so many guests in the house. 'No, no,' answered Mr Cobb, 'that is not the problem.' But he said no more.

That night after dinner when all the guests started to prepare for bed, Mr Easton, after bidding his host and hostess good-night, went up to his room. He found it very agreeable, but was still mystified by the strange conversation which had passed between the Cobbs. Mr Easton undressed and got into bed, but it seemed to him, as he later told Lord Halifax, that he had hardly fallen asleep when something strange disturbed him. There at the bottom of his bed stood the white figure of an elderly lady in the full light of the moon. She appeared to be wringing her hands and her eyes were cast down as though she was searching for something on the floor. He was not in the least afraid of the apparition for he immediately thought it was one of the guests who had mistaken her room. He sat up in bed and said, 'I beg your pardon, madam, but you have mistaken your room.' His visitor made no reply but simply vanished from sight. 'If ever there was a ghost this is one', he said to himself with an astonishing fearlessness and turned over and went to sleep.

When he came down to breakfast the next morning his host immediately asked him if he had had a good night and slept well, and seemed surprised to hear that he had. Then Mr Easton said to him, 'Oh, by the way, I had a visitor, someone in the wrong room perhaps?' He waited for his host to answer but as he said nothing, Mr Easton added, 'I am sure it was a ghost. Was that what you meant last night when you spoke about the room being a problem?'

'Yes,' said Mr Cobb, 'we never use that room if we can avoid doing so, for those friends of ours who have done so have been so terrified that they would never sleep in it again. The apparition you saw was an elderly woman, no ancestor of ours, who lived here many years ago. She was the last of her line and lived here with a child, a boy whom she knew would inherit the property, so she decided to murder him. One morning she sent the nurse out to get something she needed for the child who seems to have been delicate. During her absence she strangled the child, but in such a way that when the nurse returned and found the child dead she did not notice any signs of strangulation, and he was duly buried. It was not until the woman lay on her deathbed that she confessed her horrific crime. Had she not done so nothing would ever have been known or even suspected. After her death, my grandfather bought the property, which I inherited together with the story of the murder, which took place in the haunted room where you slept last night.'

'Do you think she will appear again tonight?' asked the artist, not a bit perturbed by the story Mr Cobb had told him.

'Certainly she will, and at about the same time.'

To the complete astonishment of his host, Mr Easton said that in that case he would like to make a sketch of her and would not wish to change his room, as had been offered to him when one of the guests departed after lunch. He spent the day painting the children and after dinner asked if he could have a lamp, which was gladly given. Once in his room he made careful arrangements for his sketch. First he put the lamp on the bedside table and turned it down very low. Then he laid out his pencils and his sketching pad and got into bed determined not to fall asleep but to keep wide awake until the elderly woman appeared once again. At precisely the same time the ghost appeared and Mr Easton, who seems to have had not only a lot of courage but a good deal of courtesy greeted her.

'Excuse me madam,' he said, sitting up in bed. 'I am an artist. Will you allow me to make a sketch of you? I shall then convince sceptics of the truth of . . . ' But at that very moment the elderly woman, who had been standing by his bed, wringing her hands and searching the floor, vanished.

It seemed quite incredible to Mr Cobb that the artist expressed a wish to stay in the room until he had completed his sketch, yet he did so for another five nights, making a week in all. Each night the ghost appeared at the same time; each night he added details to his sketch which, together with the sharp perception, retentive memory and skill of drawing which most artists possess, he put together a complete portrait of what he had seen, which he showed to Lord Halifax, who copied it and put it in his very extraordinary notebook which, regrettably, when published did not include the drawing.

Ghosts have been photographed, have been spoken to, not always as courteously as Mr Easton did, have been shot at, tackled, assaulted, even perhaps sketched from memory, but never in ghost history has an artist and a ghost had prolonged and regular meetings allowing an artist to put down for posterity definite proofs of what he had seen, nor swear to its truth and authenticity to the end of his life as did Mr Easton.

Derbyshire: 'Dickie', the Skull of Tunstead Farm

Tunstead Farm in the village of Tunstead Milton, near Chapel-en-le-Frith in Derbyshire, has for many centuries been called 'Dickie's Farm'. Though the owners of the farm for some two centuries are descendants of the Dixon family, the farmhouse has been ruled by 'Dickie', whose skull has been a resident there since the early eighteenth century, when their ancestor, Ned Dixon, returned from the wars. He was murdered in an upstairs bedroom and legend has it that his skull has been permanently kept in the room.

Another conflicting legend says that it is the skull of a woman; she also haunts the house, though who she is has never been known. The fact that the hauntings of the farm and its lands have always been attributed to 'Dickie' makes it seem more probable that the skull belonged to a male. It is almost impossible to identify since it is in three damaged parts, and there was a time when the wife of one of the tenants used to charge visitors tuppence for seeing it, an uninviting olive green object, spotted brown-and-white.

Where there are numerous references to 'Dickie's' hauntings there is only one of the unknown lady. According to Alfred Fryer, who visited the farm in the early part of the nineteenth century, the resident farmer was a Mr Lomax. He told him he had seen the lady ghost, never seen the male ghost, but had heard it countless times. It was only then that Fryer told him about 'Dickie', and Ned Dixon's murder. Mr Lomax told him how one night when he was sitting in his chair by the kitchen fire, a baby sleeping in a cradle beside his chair, he suddenly became aware of something strange in the room and turning round towards the open door he was amazed to see the figure of a woman coming slowly down the stairs and into the kitchen. Unable to move he watched her pass between him and the fire, turn and pause for a moment by the cradle, then bend over it.

For a moment he could only think that perhaps his wife had engaged a new servant, and told her not to wake the child, as he would be taking the cradle upstairs very shortly. As he began to speak the figure vanished. Very shortly after his daughter suddenly died. He told Alfred Fryer that he had never seen a ghost before, but that when he questioned the farm staff they told him they had often seen 'Dickie', as he was called even then, which seems to decide that it was a male ghost. How then could Mr Lomax have seen a woman? Clearly by its name it was recognized as a man.

The most extraordinary thing about 'Dickie' was his undisputed possession of the farm in every way. It had apparently previously bitterly resented being moved anywhere else; former tenants had been haunted by its constant presence in the house, even more so when they discovered about the murder in the bedroom, and had moved it elsewhere. As so often happens in the history of ghost skulls, once removed the noise and disturbance created in the house was so terrifying that those who had removed it would bring it back for peace and quiet.

'Dickie' had other strong objections, though these were beneficial to the farmer. If any stranger entered any of the buildings or even the land, 'Dickie' would warn the farmer by furious knockings on the walls and loud noises everywhere. Since the farm was in a very lonely part of the country this was splendid security. It was not so good though when haymaking began and the farmer was obliged to recruit new hands to help him manage the heavy work. 'Dickie' would then go quite berserk, once so terrifying two newly employed farm labourers that they fled back to wherever they had come from, unable to sleep any longer in the outbuildings to which they had been assigned.

They were replaced by three Irishmen who were put in a different part of the same outbuildings. They, too, bitterly complained that after a hard day's work in the fields they were unable to sleep. When asked why by the farmer, they told him that all through the night, in the hayloft above them, were the continuous noises of someone whetting scythes and the clattering of forks and hay-making tools being thrown about all over the floor. They got out several times in the night to try and stop the noise, but all the tools were as carefully stacked as they had placed them before going to bed. Immediately they went back to sleep the incessant racket began all over again. They too left the next day.

By that time rumours of the haunted farm were circulating. Now, however, 'Dickie' suddenly took a new and very valuable turn in his ghostly activities. Mr Lomax told Fryer that he had become a kind of watch-dog. It was first noticed when a series of deliberate and continuous noise of thuds, first loud then light and again loud, in an unvarying pattern, turned out to be a warning, for it was closely followed by a death in the family. There were other deliberate signals which were invaluable, given by knocks and raps, especially during the lambing season, or when cows were calving and needed help, sheep with footrot, horses breaking a leg, foxes endangering the chicken and even domestic cats acquiring the mange were all under the watchful care of 'Dickie'. The signals never failed and Lomax could put no value on the skull as a guardian of security.

One day the warning thuds and raps began much louder than ever before and Lomax found, to his horror, that 'Dickie' himself had been stolen. The house was full of noise. How Lomax discovered where it had gone is a mystery, but it was traced to a house in Disley, Cheshire, which became so full of noises day and night, that the robbers were only too glad to get rid of it. They secretly returned it to its home, where once again there was peace and happiness for Lomax and the skull.

The next antics of 'Dickie' gave joy to the whole of Derbyshire. One day, unannounced and unwelcome, engineers from the London and North Western Railway came to investigate the land for construction of a bridge for the London-to-Manchester line, across fields and farmlands in the nearby Goyt valley where Tunstead Farm was situated. 'Dickie' was incensed, resenting such an invasion as never before. All the efforts of the engineers to secure foundations for the erection of a bridge were repeatedly baulked. This failure was ascribed by the railway authorities to the local sand and bogs, but the Derbyshire people were certain 'Dickie' was at work. As failure after failure prevented their work, the construction engineers moved to another farm on a site near Buxton, where one of the newly built tunnels collapsed, for which 'Dickie' also received applause and credit.

It is said that one other tenant was misguided and ungrateful enough to decide that 'Dickie' should be buried in consecrated ground at 'Chapel', but such was the uproar by the locals that 'Dickie' was brought back in a basket to his home. He was reported by one writer as follows: 'among his qualifications other than that of mischief, is his immunity from decay and the fact that no dust accumulated on him', which after three centuries of his existence is hard to believe.

Apart from his exhumation from the churchyard 'Dickie' was removed from the farm on two other occasions, both of them most humiliating to him, as he soon showed. The second time he was thrown into the nearby Comb's Reservoir and caused panic by poisoning all the fish; he had hastily to be carried once more to his home. The third time was even more insulting and irreverent to 'Dickie', for when the farmhouse was being rebuilt he was thrown out into a manure heap. The workmen then found they were persistently hindered in all their tasks. Each morning, they found all the previous day's work wrecked. Angry and frustrated not only by this constant interference, but by strange and threatening noises from somewhere, they traced the noises to the manure heap where they discovered the skull. They took it back to the house, when peace was at once restored.

As late as 1938, a descendant of the original Dixon family in whose hands the farmhouse and lands were still owned and managed, told someone that when anything was likely to go wrong 'Dickie' would warn him first by various and insistent thuds and knocks on the walls, signals which never failed. He regarded 'Dickie' more as a guardian spirit of his house and family than as a terror. What more can one expect of a ghost?

Now, fifty years later, the author has been informed by a resident that rumours have been spreading that once again 'Dickie' has been thrown out, though no one knows where. There are also plans to build log-cabins around the reservoir where long ago his skull poisoned the fish, and fierce local objections are being raised. Perhaps 'Dickie' will yet again emerge from wherever he has been hidden and settle the matter of the erection of the log-cabins as he did about the railway-bridge long ago, thus bringing peace to all concerned who care so much for his welfare and believe in his own peculiar methods of resurrection.

Lincolnshire: Old Jeffery of Epworth Parsonage

When John Wesley, the founder of Methodism, made an authentic, truthful documentation of the activities of the ghost in his father's parsonage at Epworth in Lincolnshire, he could never have guessed that it would become a classic of its kind. The ghost fell upon the house in December 1716 with a speed as sudden as its departure only two months later in January 1717. During that dramatic short period it brought to every single member of that very numerous family, and its staff, nothing but mystery, anxiety, and fear. John Wesley was convinced that it was a judgement of God for a rash and cruel vow his father had made some fifteen years earlier, though why the Divine punishment was so long withheld is yet another mystery.

It was in the year 1701 when the family, assembled as usual at six o'clock in the evening for prayers, heard the Reverend Samuel Wesley make his vow. 'The year before King William died,' wrote his son John:

My father observed my mother did not say 'Amen' to his prayers for the king. She said she would not, for she did not believe that William was more than Prince of Orange and no lawful King of England. My father vowed he would not cohabit with her until she did. He then took his horse and rode away, nor did she hear anything of him for a twelve-month. He then came back and lived with her as before. But I fear his vow was not forgotten before God.

This stubborn and selfish act might well have given his wife some respite from his great virility, for he managed to father no less than nineteen children, John being the first one to be born after the reconciliation. His father had never at any time been popular with people in his parish, or even

beyond, because of his political views. The people had
always supported the Stuart cause, whereas Wesley was an
adherent of William III and the Hanoverians. So without
any compunction at all they burnt down the parsonage in
1709, though it was rebuilt in brown brick before the end of
the year.

John Wesley was about thirteen when the ghost made its
first visitation. It was on 2 December, about ten o'clock at
night, when it suddenly began its activities. Robert Brown,
manservant to the Reverend Wesley, was sitting in the
dining-room with one of the maids when they were astonished to hear knocking on the door. Robert rose to open it
but no one was there. He had just sat down again when
there was more knocking, this time accompanied by groaning. 'It is Mr Turpin,' said Robert, 'he used to groan so.' He
opened the door three more times, and still there was no
one there. By now they were both startled and puzzled but
they went off to bed, Brown, as was his custom, taking off
his boots downstairs before retiring.

As Robert reached the top of the stairs to go to his attic
room he was astonished to see a handmill whirling about,
though there was no one there to do the grinding. When he
told his story the next morning he said: 'I thought if it had
been but full of malt he might have ground his hand out for
me.' A dour sense of humour indeed for one who was
undoubtedly scared out of his wits, even more so when he
had got into bed where, close to the bedside, he heard the
loud gobbling of a turkey-cock, followed by someone
stumbling about on the floor.

When he and the maid told the dairymaid of the continual knocking on the door the night before, she laughed
mockingly: 'What a couple of fools you are! I defy anything
to fright me.' After the evening churning she put the butter
on a tray to carry it into the dairy when a loud knocking
came from the shelf on which the puncheons of milk stood.
She began to search with a lighted candle, but as the knocking grew louder she fled from the dairy in sheer terror.

From these first visitations the ghost began an almost
daily and systematic purging of every member of both the

Wesley household and its staff. It became so puzzling and
so serious that the Reverend Samuel Wesley began to
record its appearances. It was from his diary, and the letters
his mother wrote to his eldest brother, recording the
minutest details, that John Wesley collated it all, accur-
ately, minutely and truthfully.

One of the most interesting sides to the haunting is the
way life was lived in that parsonage under its strict and
stubborn parson, who fathered year after year another
child, nearly always a daughter. There were a cat and a big
dog. There was a duty roster for the daughters. Every night
one of them had to sit outside her parents' bedroom until
the Reverend Samuel was in bed and called out. Then the
daughter would enter and take away the lighted candle.
There were the evening prayers. There were stables, a
dairy, many rooms, and the regular routine of a country
parsonage which had never altered one jot until the ghost
came to spreadeagle it all.

On the second night, between five and six o'clock,
Molly, one of the daughters, sat reading in the dining-
room. She suddenly heard the door from the hall open and
a person entered who seemed to be wearing a trailing,
rustling silk nightgown or dress. It walked all around her,
then to the door and back again, but since the ghost was
invisible she saw nothing at all. She decided it was no good
showing her fear by running away, as whatever it was
could certainly move faster than she, so she got up quite
calmly, put her book under her arm and walked out of the
room. After supper, when they were in their bedroom, she
told her younger sister Sukey what she had experienced,
but jestingly. Even as she spoke, a knocking began under
the table, but she saw no one there. Then the iron casement
began clattering. In spite of her previous mocking Molly,
now quite scared, jumped into one of the beds without
undressing and pulled the clothes over her head, not
daring to move until morning.

A night or two later, Hetty, another sister, was waiting
outside her father's door between nine and ten at night
when her parents had gone to bed, waiting for her father to

call her in and give her the candlestick and lighted candle. She distinctly heard heavy steps coming down the staircase from the attic towards and past her, the steps almost shaking the house. With the candle she had just taken from her father held high she moved as fast as she could along the passage and into her own room, and covered her head with the bedclothes.

When she told her eldest sister Emilia the next morning, she laughed aloud, though not revealing that she herself had heard noises. 'I don't believe a word of it. I'll take the candle tonight and so will find out the truth.'

My sisters [Hetty later wrote to her brother John] heard noises and told me of them, but I did not much believe till one night just after the clock struck ten I went downstairs to lock the doors, which I always do. Scarce had I got up the west stairs when I heard a noise like a person throwing down a vast coal in the middle of the kitchen. I was not much frightened but went to my sister Sukey and we together went over all the lower rooms, and there was nothing out of order. Our dog was fast asleep and our cat in the other end of the house. No sooner was I got upstairs and undressing for bed, but I heard a noise. This made me hasten to bed.

The next night Emilia herself waited outside her father's door for the candle. She had just come from the room with it when she heard a loud banging in the hall below and went downstairs at once. But when she reached the hall, the banging began in the kitchen; when she went there, the knocking began on the kitchen door outside, but when she dared to open it there was no one outside. Immediately she closed the door the knocking came again. Once more she cautiously opened it, only to find herself pushed violently against the wall by the door she was holding. After a quite desperate struggle she finally closed the door and locked it, though the knocking at once began again. Even all her scepticism vanished before the fear she now had as she rushed back upstairs to her room, too frightened even to wake anyone.

The next morning she gave a full account of her experience to her mother, who simply replied, 'If I hear anything myself I shall know how to judge,' and went on with her work. She did not say that she was all the time relating each separate incident in every letter she wrote to her eldest son Samuel in London. The most incomprehensible thing is that her husband seemed totally unaware of what was going on in his own house until the following incident occurred.

Two or three days later, Emilia burst into a room where her mother was, urgently begging her to come at once to the nursery from which a strange noise was coming. As they reached the door they could both hear a sound as if a cradle was being violently rocked on the wooden floor, although there had been no cradle there for years. Mrs Wesley was frightened and now fully convinced that the supernatural had entered the parsonage. She tried to expel it by long and earnest prayers. Finally she thought it right to tell her husband. His reaction was one of violent anger. 'I am ashamed of you,' he shouted. 'These boys and girls frighten one another, but you are a woman of sense and should know better. Let me hear of it no more!' – and he stormed out of the room.

That very evening his own turn came. The whole household had assembled for evening prayers as usual. When the Reverend Samuel began the prayer for the king a violent knocking began and continued all round the room. Every evening session of prayer was rudely interrupted immediately the prayer for the king began by the most loud and violent knocking. It must finally have come home to the parson that God at least had not forgotten the vow he had taken all those years ago. He conceded nothing to his wife, but such was his apprehension that he decided to seek help and advice from another clergyman, a Mr Hoole, the vicar of nearby Haxey. He sent his manservant Robert Brown to request the vicar to come to the parsonage as soon as he could. He then gave a full account of all the disturbances, particularly the most recent and continuous thundering on the walls during the prayer for the king.

That very evening there was no disturbance at all throughout the prayers. Between nine and ten, however, a servant came into the room where the two clergymen sat talking and said, 'Old Jeffery is coming for I hear the signal.' This name had been given to the ghost by the children as a joke because another man bearing it had died in the house long before they came, though their father had no knowledge of this. The signal of Old Jeffery's visit was regular in time and place, as John Wesley wrote:

It was towards the top of the house, on the outside, at the north-east corner, resembling the loud creaking of a saw, or rather that of a windmill when the body of it is turned about in order to shift the sails to the wind.

Almost at that very moment the knocking began above them. 'Come, sir,' said the Reverend Wesley, taking up the lighted candle, 'now you shall hear for yourself.' With no little fear the vicar followed the parson upstairs to the nursery. As they went in the knocking began in the next room, and when they entered that it returned to the nursery. During this shuttling to and fro the three children put to sleep there were greatly alarmed, particularly Hetty, who lay trembling and sweating with fear.

The Reverend Wesley, whose temper was always short, became very angry indeed, and to the vicar's horror he drew a pistol from his belt and pointed it at the headboard of Hetty's bed, threatening to shoot the ghost if it did not stop its knocking. The vicar, now more afraid of Wesley than of the ghost, snatched at his extended arm as he raised it to fire, 'Sir, you are so convinced this is something supernatural. If so you cannot hurt it, but you give it power to hurt you.' Wesley lowered the pistol, but still shaking with anger went right up to the bedboard and in a stern, threatening voice addressed the spirit.

'Thou deaf and dumb devil! Why dost thou fright these children who cannot answer for themselves? Come to me in my study, that am a man!' Instantly the spirit knocked the parson's own familiar knock, which he always used at the gate to announce his arrival, so powerfully that it almost splintered the headboard. Then it was silent.

What is always so astonishing in all the stories of hauntings is that any child was able to avoid a breakdown. To think of three children in a nursery with their father bending over them holding a loaded pistol, another strange man beside him, and the knowledge that there was indeed a ghost in the house is almost incredible.

The Reverend Wesley's challenge to the spirit was soon taken up, for the very next evening as he attempted to go into his study, to which only he had a key, the door opened with such violence that he was nearly knocked down. Then the thundering knocks began again, first on one wall, then on another, then in the next room where another daughter, Nancy, was sitting. He went at once to her and told her to put out the candle. 'These spirits love darkness,' he said, 'perhaps it will speak.' The knocking went on and he said to Nancy, 'Nancy, two Christians are an overmatch for the devil. Go downstairs. It may be when I am alone he will have courage to speak.'

When he was alone in the darkness he spoke aloud: 'If thou art the spirit of my son Samuel, I pray you knock three knocks and no more.' Immediately there was silence. It was a troubled man indeed who went out of the room, for the ghost had now switched its attacks from the children to him. The knocking went on wherever he was, day and night. His mastiff dog always gave warning seconds before the disturbance began. As John Wesley wrote:

My father was thrice pushed by an invisible power, once against the corner of his bed, then against the door of the matted chamber, a third time against his study door. His dog always gave warning by running whining towards him, though he no longer barked at it as he did the first time.

Then the spirit, ghost, or poltergeist, whatever it was, made its first visible appearance. Mrs Wesley first saw a shape 'like a badger but without any head' which seemed to run under Emily's petticoats. A servant later saw the same shape in the dining-room before it ran out past him into the hall. He saw it again a few days later in the kitchen, but thought it looked like a rabbit. Whatever it was it became most persistent, incessantly running up and down the stairs, making strange cries like the gobbling of a turkey. Then a maid heard a terrible noise as of a death-rattle, and was so terrified she could not even move from the room.

Other strange things began, such as the lifting of door latches. Once when Emily tried to hold one down with all her strength it still was not enough to stop it. The Reverend Wesley was more and more interrupted while at prayer by loud banging, knocking, and other noises. He would follow the sounds from room to room but never saw anything. It became more and more unnerving, and he would sit alone in his study for long periods of time trying to commune with the spirit to find out what it wanted him to do. He was never once answered articulately, though about three times he heard little squeaks, as if from an animal. Hetty, too, was suffering acutely, trembling and sweating in her sleep, her breathing difficult, her face flushed, and very restless before, during, and after Old Jeffery's visitations.

One night when the Reverend Wesley and his wife had gone to bed and the candle had not been taken away, they heard three heavy blows, repeated twice and thrice, as if someone were beating a heavy oak club on a chest beside their bed. Wesley rose and taking the candle went to the door, his wife by his side. There were now great noises below and together they went down the stairs. John Wesley wrote:

There was a sound as if a vessel full of silver was poured upon my mother's breast, and ran jingling down to her feet. Quickly after there was the sound of a large iron bell being thrown among many bottles under the stairs. Soon after our large mastiff dog came and ran to shelter himself between them. While the disturbances continued he would bark, leap, and snap on one side and the other. Then it seemed as if a very large coal was violently thrown upon the floor and dashed all in pieces, but nothing was seen. My father cried out: 'Sukey, do you not hear? All the pewter is thrown about the kitchen.' But when they looked all the pewter stood in place.

Then there was knocking at the back door but no one was there. Next it went to the front door, back again, to and fro. Finally, they decided to go back to their bed but not to sleep, for the bangs, knocking, and other violent noises continued throughout the night as they lay terrified in their bed. The details of all the ghost's activities began to circulate, not only in the village but far beyond. Friends, acquaintances, parishioners, and other clergymen all begged the Reverend Wesley to quit the house, but he stubbornly refused as it had now become a struggle he must win.

'No,' he remonstrated to all who tried to reason with him. 'No! Let the devil flee from me, I will never flee from the devil.' But at last he wrote to his eldest son Samuel in London, asking him to come to Epworth. This, more than anything else indicated his own great fear at last. His son was about to leave when another letter reached him saying that finally all the disturbances were over and there was peace.

It may well be that the Reverend Wesley felt he had won a great victory over the devil, as befitted his creed and his profession. It may be that his son John was right in believing it was a judgement from God for his vow and that the punishment was now considered to have been sufficient. But all the evidence is in John Wesley's story in the *Arminian Magazine* of 1784, written sixty-four years after the ghost had gone, and when he himself was over eighty. It is concise, clear, abundant, and the whole document is stamped with the truth of all the people concerned. It remains not only a classic but an insoluble mystery which has baffled every single expert who has tried to solve it.

Oxfordshire: Ghosts at Magdalen College

As late as February 1987, Magdalen College, Oxford had an invasion of ghostly noises, whisperings, footsteps and even apparitions which brought terror to one girl, dispelled all doubts in other students who did not believe in ghosts, and caused numerous problems in the college. Such was the terror of the female language student that the Reverend Jeffrey John considered it advisable to bless her room, as well as others, by offering prayers to bring peace and quiet to the restless souls haunting the college.

The college was founded in 1458 by Bishop Waynflete, Bishop of Winchester. The original site on which it was built included the thirteenth-century St John's Hospital, whose buildings extended east as far as the river. In 1294 the brethren were given permission for their burial-ground to be on the south side of the road, doubtless the old burial-place of the Jews, who had been banished from England. In 1335 it is written that the brethren and sisters quarrelled a lot. In 1341 a certain Alice complained that the king had given her sustenance for life from the hospital, but that the Master and certain citizens of Oxford had assaulted her and taken the document. It had been endowed by the king 'for the relief of poor scholars and other miserable persons', to be governed by a Master elected by the brethren; there was to be a cellarer and a sacrist, the latter to have charge of the infirmary and to hear confessions. Incurable cases were not to be received and the hospital was exempt from episcopal and archidiaconal visits. In 1320 the Archbishop visiting Oxford was told not to meddle in the business of the hospital.

It was, therefore, quite understandable who were 'the lost souls' the Dean was praying for, because he, like many others in the College, were convinced that the monks were trying to escape from the uproar and noise of the archaeological 'dig' being carried out by the Oxford Archaeological Unit before construction of new kitchens for the present-day college. But even before this, there had been hauntings in the college, as reported in *Isis* on 5 June 1968, when one Sunday morning very early, a student who was walking across the dew-soaked college lawn towards the Colonnade arches saw with astonishment a black-clad figure moving from the cloisters towards him. He said that the figure glided rather than walked in complete silence and with no movement of the gown it wore. The student stared hard at it, but where its head should have been, he saw only the wooden door twenty yards further on leading to the arches. Even when the figure walked on the stone pavement, its footsteps were noiseless. As it came into a stronger light on reaching the entrance to the staircase it vanished. In explaining what he had seen to the *Isis* reporter, he said the whole thing defeated all his rational faculties.

Only a few weeks earlier a first-year historian, who had stated he was 'as cynical about ghosts as it is possible to be', crossed the same lawn one night between eleven and twelve o'clock. He saw to his left what is called a 'fetch', explaining he saw 'a black silhouette keeping pace with me as I walked towards the colonnades. The figure kept pace exactly with me and I kept glancing to my left to look at it. There was no sound of footsteps. We went up the few steps under the arches together; it was about ten yards away. When I looked to my left after passing under the arch and into the colonnade, I expected to see it still keeping pace with me, but it had completely disappeared'. It was only later, when he happened to hear about the first student's sight of the apparition that he, also, was forced 'to have all his rational faculties defied' and he could offer no explanation of the phenomenon. It transpired later that many other students had seen the black figure on that same lawn and all were equally puzzled, forced to believe there must be 'something'.

The latest apparition that appeared, on Friday the 13th of February 1987 (of all days), was far more terrifying than the silent black figure familiar to many students, for it struck terror into Catriona Oliphant, a 26-year-old language student. She was sleeping late that morning when she was awakened by sounds of mysterious whisperings and then frightened by seeing the locked door of her room opening and feeling a strong physical 'presence' moving towards her and leaning over her. She was too terrified even to scream and only when it disappeared was she able to move and rush down to a friend's room near her own. So great was the shock that she was obliged to sleep the next two nights in the sickroom of the college. She did not return until Dr Jeffrey John, Magdalen's Dean of Divinity, had decided to quieten the lost souls by offering prayers.

Two other undergraduates spoke of a haunted staircase on which they had seen a dark figure crawling across the carpet in their rooms at night. Another girl student had heard singing, footsteps and moving furniture in the next room where the occupant was sleeping soundly and heard nothing. Other students reported hearing noises in locked rooms which, when opened by the college porter showed no signs at all of any disturbance, even pillows on the beds being unruffled. Mr Strutt, the head porter, reported that on Christmas Day 1978, when the college was empty, he had been doing a security check when he saw a figure ahead. Rapidly moving forward to ask him what he was doing there, the figure vanished just as he was about to hold him.

Since starting work at the college six months earlier, in 1986, Mr Gordon Hallam said he had often heard heavy footsteps above the lodge where he was on duty and when he knew that the rooms were locked. He had often heard strange noises, sometimes twice a week, sometimes not for a month or more, but did not seem to be unduly scared.

When Father John was asked what he thought of all these strange manifestations, he said that there was no doubt at all in his mind that the students were quite genuine about what they had seen. 'There have been stories connected with this part of the college for centuries,' he said, 'it is unlikely that these things are disturbed by being dug up but it seemed to me to be the right thing to go and say some prayers.' The Reverend Brian Findlay, who was Dean of Divinity at Magdalen from 1975 to 1984, was not so sure. 'A lot of manifestations that people describe as hauntings are often connected with people rather than places or build-

ings. I just don't understand at all. I just have to step in and
do what I can. Sometimes the phenomenon can be frightening, and physically very damaging.'

Dr Ian Burrow, Director of the Archaeological Unit, said
that reports of ghosts had come as a complete surprise. 'If
we have disturbed ghosts,' he said, 'it is better to have
done it now rather than when building contractors start
work in June during students' exams.' It can only be hoped
that the Dean's prayers for the lost souls will decide the
matter and bring peace to everybody in Magdalen College.

Shropshire: *The Angry Ghost of Kinlet*

One of the angriest ghosts is surely that of Sir George
Blount of Kinlet in Shropshire. The Blounts were a very
ancient and distinguished family dating back as far as the
Norman Conquest. Their original name would probably
have been Blond, for they were all fair-haired, with bright
blue eyes and ruddy complexions. Highly connected as
they were in the royal courts, the most famous of the family
was Sir George's sister, Bessie Blount. She was a most
beautiful girl and her first appearance at Henry VIII's court
was when she was twelve. She later became Lady-in-
Waiting to Katharine of Aragon. It was not long before
Henry fell in love with her, resulting in her bearing the
King's child, the future Duke of Richmond and Somerset.
She was never spoken of as the royal mistress, but always
as 'The mother of the king's son'.

Sir George's tomb in Kinlet church has been described
by church historians as one of the finest and noblest monuments in England, a magnificent example of Elizabethan
architecture. He is shown with his wife and his two
children John and Dorothy. John died quite young, choked
by the 'scork' of an apple, the Shropshire word for core. It
was Dorothy who all unwittingly became the sole reason
for her father's ghost, who not only haunted his fine
mansion Kinlet Hall, near the church, but almost the whole
area of Kinlet.

Sir George, as squire of Kinlet and Bewdley, was a very
rich man. An aristocrat and a man to be feared if anyone
crossed swords with him. Local people held various views
of him: he has been described as affable and courteous by
some and as quarrelsome and bad-tempered by others. His
later conduct towards his only daughter seems to support
the latter opinion.

There are two accounts of his outburst of fury and ulti-
mate revenge when he was told, either by Dorothy herself
or by others, that she was going to be married. It must be
remembered that in those days, and especially in great
families like the Blounts, the sharp and inviolable division
of class was the most important thing in the arrangement of
any marriage, because with a daughter there was the question of the disposal of her dowry, so that if she died before
her marriage, the dowry did not go to her fiancé. It was also
an accepted fact that such marriages were arranged by the
parents, who chose the bride or bridegroom for their sons
and daughters when they were tiny children and had never
met their future wives or husbands. There was never any
question of just falling in love, and a family would never
consider marrying into another beneath them in class and
rank.

The first story, and the authentic one, is that when
Dorothy informed Sir George that she was going to be
married to a Mr John Parslowe she 'had the misfortune
mortally to offend her father in the tenderest point'. As sole
heiress of his estate she had shown a remarkable disregard
of her father's pride about rank and title. In his eyes, she
had flouted him by marrying a neighbouring country
gentleman of no rank, who also was a widower. Mr
Parslowe later died, leaving Dorothy a widow.

Sir George was determined that her substantial dowry
would not pass to her husband. He disinherited Dorothy
and passed the whole of his estate to the children of his
sister Agnes. Why he deserted the male line by passing
over his nephew is not easily understood considering his
pride of lineage, more especially since his nephew was

George Blount, his namesake, and the son of his brother Henry.

The second story is legendary, but has passed into Shropshire folklore, described by a local as *Squire Blount's Ghost Story*. When Dorothy had 'become a young woman' she fell in love with a page-boy in Kinlet Hall, which must have required great skill and cunning on both sides to conceal this, especially from her father. Another man loved her, but whenever the page-boy opened the door to him he said that Dorothy was not at home, as she had instructed the page-boy to say. As the visits continued and the page-boy's story was always the same, suspicion grew. As a result Dorothy and the page-boy were married, presumably after eloping, although that is not stated. The marriage was strengthened financially by Dorothy's conviction that her dowry would be secure and given to her husband once she had won her father over.

When Sir George discovered what had happened his anger was uncontrollable. He told her that not only would she not have a dowry, but not even his estate on his death. More than that, he put a curse on her and all her descendants swearing that he would haunt her during her whole lifetime and long after that if there were any children.

His first appearance as a ghost was in a large pool near Kinlet Hall where the women used to 'swill' their clothes. They grew more and more terrified as each day saw the return of Squire Blount, mounted on horseback and charging out of the pool straight at them, before vanishing. One by one the women ceased to bring their clothes there to wash them until at last no one came at all. The ghost continued to come until many years later the pool dried up altogether, but it is still known as Blount's Pool even today.

His ghost then attacked his old home Kinlet Hall with such ferocity and persistence that it had to be pulled down and another house built in 1720. He would appear at all hours of the day and night seated in his coach, driving the four horses at breakneck speed through the rooms, even over the dinner-table as Dorothy and her husband and guests sat there. At other times he would appear alone in his cellars which had been filled with countless bottles of fine wine and brandy, hogsheads of ale and beer. No one dared go down and touch the bottles for fear of what he might do to them. At last priests were called in to exorcize his spirit and bring peace to both him and those he haunted.

In a very strange ceremony, the priests, after a long consultation, lit a number of candles which they placed upon the long refectory table. They then read a special service from 'Books of magic' until only one candle was left burning, beside which they placed a flat glass bottle. At the moment the candle-flame guttered and went out, they believed that Squire Blount's spirit entered the bottle and they stoppered it down, carried it into the church and placed it by his tomb, certain they had at last quietened his spirit and liberated it from any more angry and revengeful haunting. Children were most solemnly warned never to touch it for fear of Old Squire Blount coming back again. Peace reigned in Kinlet and the surrounding countryside, and one day the bottle disappeared.

In August 1883, two young women aged 18 and 24, when visiting the church actually saw the bottle and told one of their school friends about it, who suggested pulling out the stopper to see what was inside. The others were so terrified at what would happen that they all ran out of the church. Some three years later, other visitors, who were very reliable, testified to seeing the unstoppered bottle which appeared to contain some chemical liquid used for photography. After that, the bottle really did disappear, presumably taking Squire Blount's ghost somewhere else.

4 The North

Cumbria: The Radiant Boy of Corby Castle

One of the most beautiful legends of a quiet ghost is surely that of the Radiant Boy who once haunted Corby Castle. The fine eighteenth-century castle on the banks of the River Eden is near Carlisle in Cumbria. The first recorded entry of the appearance of the Radiant Boy was in an entry dated 3 September 1803 taken from a journal by a Mrs Crowe, who published it in her book *The Night Side of Nature*, concerning the strange behaviour not of the ghost but of the Rector of Greystoke, who, with his wife, had been invited as guests to the castle to stay for several days, with many other guests:

According to previous arrangements the Rector and his wife were to have remained several days but their visit was cut short in a very unexpected manner. On the morning after their arrival we were all assembled at breakfast when a chaise-and-four dashed up to the door in such haste that it knocked down part of the fence of my flower garden. Our curiosity was of course awakened to know who could be arriving at so early an hour, when, happening to turn my eyes towards Mr A- (*he was the rector*) I observed that he appeared extremely agitated. 'It is our carriage', said he. 'I am very sorry, but we must absolutely leave you this morning' . . . . The breakfast was no sooner over than they departed, leaving us in consternation to conjecture what could have possibly occasioned so sudden an alteration in their arrangements.

This account goes on at some length but at last the writer was in a district near to the Rector and they met each other again which resulted in a full explanation of his conduct that morning when he left Corby Castle in such haste.

Soon after we went to bed we fell asleep. It might be between one and two in the morning when I awoke. I observed that the fire was totally extinguished; but although that was the case, and we had no light, I saw a glimmer in the middle of the room, which suddenly increased to a bright flame. I looked out, apprehending that something had caught fire; when to my amazement, I beheld a beautiful boy clothed in white, with bright locks resembling gold, standing by my bedside, in which position he remained some minutes, fixing his eyes upon me with a mild and benevolent expression. He then glided gently towards the side of the chimney; where it is obvious there is no possible egress, and entirely disappeared. I found myself again in total darkness, and all remained quiet until the usual hour of rising, I declare this to be a true account of what I saw at Corby Castle, upon my word as a clergyman.

The haunted room formed part of the old house, with windows looking into the court which was designed in early times as security against the enemy. The haunted room in question 'is by no means remote or solitary, being surrounded on all sides by chambers that are constantly inhabited. It is accessible by a passage cut through a wall eight feet in thickness, and its dimensions are twenty-one feet by eighteen'. The walls were covered with tapestries and family pictures to relieve the gloom of the unaccountable reports of apparitions and extraordinary noises which were constantly being received from guests. The writer states 'But I regret to say I did not succeed in banishing the nocturnal visitor which still continues to disturb our friends.' He then confirms the clergyman's story which had been circulating a long time.

What is interesting about the journal entries is the mention of apparitions in the plural as well as noises but no individual mention of the Radiant Boy seen by the Rector, who heard no noises at all and was able to give a detailed account of only one phantom. How was it that he was not warned of the room being haunted and, stranger still, how was it that so quiet, so mild and so beautiful a ghost terrified him so much that he left in such speed the next morning? And more mysterious still is the fact that there is only mention of one other anywhere in ghost histories of a Radiant Boy, who he was or why he haunted Corby Castle.

Strangely enough, Mrs Crowe was responsible for another story of a Radiant Boy who haunted a room in which Captain Robert Stewart, later Lord Castlereagh, then becoming the second Marquis of Londonderry KG, slept in what is described very vaguely 'as a house in the north of Ireland', where as a young man he happened to be quartered. He was fond of sport and while out shooting had completely lost his way; with the weather worsening he sought shelter at the house of a gentleman, who, with true Irish hospitality, welcomed him warmly. In offering a bed for the night, he explained that others as well had sought shelter from the weather for the night, but he would make him as comfortable as possible. After a jolly evening with the many other guests he was conducted to a room, sparse of furniture but with a blazing peat fire and a shakedown on the floor, made up of cloaks and various material. Captain Stewart was tired after his energetic day, but thought it advisable to take some of the peat off the fire before retiring. The story then goes on:

He believed he had slept about a couple of hours, when he awoke suddenly, and was startled by such a vivid light in the room that he thought it was on fire; but, on turning to look at the grate, he saw the fire was out, though it was from the chimney the light proceeded. He sat up in bed, trying to discover what it was, when he perceived, gradually disclosing itself, the form of a beautiful naked boy, surrounded by a dazzling radiance. The boy looked at him, earnestly, and then the vision faded, and all was dark.

Captain Stewart was indignant, thinking someone was playing a practical joke on him and took care to express anger to his host and the other guests at breakfast next morning. His host asked the butler which room Captain Stewart had occupied and when told it was *The Boy's Room* was very angry, telling the butler that he had had strict instructions never to put anyone in that room, ignoring the butler's protest that there was no other free room.

The host then went back to Captain Stewart, apologized, and told him the story of the Radiant Boy. The family tradition was that whoever the Radiant Boy appeared to would rise to great heights, but when he had reached the climax of these things he would die a violent death. Gravely and impressively the host added, 'records that have been kept of his appearance go to confirm this persuasion.'

Every word of this came true for few men have reached the distinguished heights Viscount Castlereagh attained during his lifetime, but towards the end of his career he became ill with gout, became terribly depressed and fears were felt for his reason. He finally sought medical help on the advice of the Duke of Wellington and went to his home in North Cray Place, near Dartford in Kent, where he committed suicide by cutting his throat with a penknife, his razors having been taken away from him on the doctor's advice.

Cumbria: *The Ghost Army of Souter Fell*

It was late evening on Midsummer Eve 1735 that a farm-hand, working in the fields suddenly stopped, looking across them to the Fells. His unbelieving eyes were concentrated on the top of Souter or Soutra Fell where he saw, almost with terror, what looked like part of a huge army crossing from east to west, where after long minutes it disappeared in a cleft in the mountainside.

Souter Fell, on the left-hand side of the Keswick-Penrith road, is above the path leading from the village of Scales to the mountain of Saddleback, 2,847 feet. The farm-hand knew the Fells well and knew that Souter Fell was some 900 feet high, the north and west sides were sheer precipices, and it was impossible for a number of people to move on the summit, let alone an army. As it began to grow darker he moved back towards Mr Lancaster's farm where he worked some half-a-mile away from the Fells. His story of what he had seen was scornfully, almost insultingly ridiculed, even more so when it was jeeringly passed on by the farmer to the villagers.

Two years later, again on Midsummer Eve, it was not the farm-hand but Mr Lancaster and his family who witnessed exactly what his farm-hand had described to him and what he had totally disbelieved, even mocked at. At first he saw only a number of men leading their horses and for a moment thought they might be huntsmen, except that he knew only too well no hunt could possibly take place at that height. Some ten minutes or so later they were followed by what seemed to be a cavalry regiment riding five abreast under the leadership of officers who rode up and down the ranks of cavalry and the following army of marching soldiers. The whole procession passed towards the cleft in the mountainside and vanished. As twilight came on and clouds gathered above the Fells, they had only time to see some stragglers trying to catch up with the army before darkness fell, and the family turned back home. It was now their turn to be insulted by the villagers to whom they told their astonishing story, none of the listeners believed them even though the Fells, and Souter Fell in particular, were renowned for legends and superstitions handed down through the centuries.

Each successive year, however, the Lancaster family went out on Midsummer Eve to see once again the ghost army, but nothing happened until the tenth year after the first sighting by the farm-hand. It was 1745, the fateful year of the Jacobite Rebellion in Scotland. This time the Lancasters had summoned twenty-six other people, determined that their own story could be justified and this time believed. What they all saw was unimaginable, for a vast army of marching soldiers, stretching for at least half-a-mile, passed over the summit of Souter Fell. This time a number of carriages were seen, though everybody watching knew only too well that not even one carriage could move across. The long procession of infantry, cavalry and carriages seemed endless until, as darkness fell, nothing more was visible and the dumbfounded, incredulous watchers went silently home. The very next day, still disbelieving what they themselves had now seen, some of the party climbed up Souter Fell to see the hoof marks of the cavalry and the wheel tracks of the carriages, but there was nothing to be seen anywhere as evidence that such a vast army had passed there only a few hours before. So convinced were they all by now that each one of them swore on oath before a magistrate that what he or she had witnessed was the truth. More strangely still they were now supported by others, no longer afraid to tell what they had seen of other spectres, for fear of being insulted as the Lancasters had been.

One of these was a Mr Wren of Wilton Hall. One summer evening in 1743 he, with a farm-hand, had seen on a dangerous and precipitous part of Souter Fell where nothing was safe, a man and his dog, chasing at a tremendous pace some wild horses, and were sure that all must inevitably have been killed.

In other counties, there have also been ghost armies reported to have been seen on heights, always on Midsummer Eve, notably the giant figure of King Arthur at the head of his cavalry, all in full armour, their lance tips glittering in the sunlight, riding down from Cadbury Fort in Somerset, to water their horses at a well, still known as Arthur's Well. Legend or not, the people of Somerset living near the fort have solemnly sworn they have seen the army of ghosts. One villager of a great age swore on oath that he had picked up a silver horseshoe near the well after the cavalry had departed.

Explanations of the army of ghosts on Souter Fell have been offered, such as visions, mirages, reflected light and transparent vapour, but all these were totally unacceptable to the Lancaster family and their witnesses. They were convinced that the vast army they had seen with their own eyes was real, and it is their firm belief which has passed into the folklore and legends of the Lake District.

Lancashire: *The Dubious Skull of Wardley Hall*

It is a great pity that the magnificent quadrangular, wood, plaster and brick building called Wardley Hall has become known as *The Skull House*. It was built in the reign of Henry VI on the site of an older house, whose moat and gatehouse still remain. This unattractive title is solely due to the legend of its far-famed and gruesome skull contained in a recess at the head of the main staircase since the reign of Charles II and quite erroneously believed to be that of Roger Downes.

Whatever the original legend, it has been so distorted, falsified and exploited that all the versions have become totally unconvincing. All that is certain is that the skull belonged to a man with a bitter and stubborn resistance against its removal to anywhere else but where it now is. If anyone dared to remove it chaos would ensue.

Wardley Hall in Greater Manchester belonged to the Worsleys and then the Tildesleys until the seventeenth century, when it passed into the possession of the Downes family, whose arms may still be seen on the staircase, near what has always been accepted as Roger Downes' skull. That belief was shattered when, in 1779, his coffin was opened and found to contain his full skeleton, after which rumours never ceased to spread and guesses multiplied alarmingly as to whose skull it really was.

Roger Downes was a particularly unpleasant man during his lifetime, a debauchee, a boaster and swaggerer, aggressive and quarrelsome, one of Charles II's loose-living cronies. He was known as a 'scourer', one who swaggered about the streets of London looking for unarmed and defenceless people whom they could attack with their sword, slicing off an ear or slitting a nose for the sheer delight it gave them as sport. Even 'the watch' though armed themselves, forerunners of the police force today, avoided them whenever possible, because the royal privilege overlooked any crime a 'scourer' might commit.

At last there came a night when the tide turned against Downes. It was on London Bridge, according to one version. He made an attack on one of the watchmen, who seemed to him to be the feeblest, instead of which he was suddenly confronted by a very tough man indeed, who attacked him with his halberd and severing his head from his body, the head rolled into the gutter.

The second version of his death is that Downes and some of his cronies were having great sport with some fiddlers whom they had caught. They began tossing them in a blanket higher and higher, meaning to snatch the blanket away so that the fiddlers would then crash on to the cobbled street. Their sport was suddenly interrupted by the watch who had been called to the affray by a bystander. Lord Rochester, another crony of Charles II, drew his sword and attacked one of the watchmen, but Downes sprang forward and saved the man's life. He himself, however, was felled by another watchman and so badly wounded that he died a few days later. His body was buried in Wigan church.

In the first version there is no mention of a burial; instead it is said that Downes' head was picked up from the gutter, put into a box and sent back to Wardley Hall as a present for his sister Penelope, who was later married to Richard Savage, Earl Rivers. It was she who put the skull in the recess at the head of the staircase, where it has been ever since. It is quite incredible that the watch should have sent the skull back, for the long journey from London Bridge to Wardley Hall would have been very expensive and certainly not paid for by any of the watchmen, even if they knew who it was. The skull has remained where she put it ever since, except for one or two absences.

It was Penelope who caused the first of these absences for, with the best intentions in the world, she decided her brother's skull should have a Christian burial and be committed to the churchyard. All the arrangements were made for this and the skull in its box was taken down and put into the care of the priest overnight, ready for the burial service the next morning. However Penelope, had not consulted the skull, for scarcely had it left Wardley Hall than it asserted itself with great force. That very night a storm of such power broke over the house that those who were living there fled in terror from room to room. They hid under beds and in corners as the storm raged above the Hall as if it had been singled out for destruction. It did not end until dawn broke. Downes' sister, convinced that the skull was the whole cause of the havoc, hastily fetched it back and returned it to the head of the staircase, when immediate silence came and peace was restored. Later, there were other occasions when tenants had moved it out of the house; almost at once havoc would break out again. It was evident that the skull ruled the Hall to such an extent that no one ever dared to move it again.

Whilst all this is a good story of horror and skull-power, which has been repeated in other houses, notably Burton Agnes in Yorkshire and Chilton Cantelo in Somerset, nothing has substantiated the truth. In an effort to settle the matter, in 1779 an unnamed tenant of the house unable to live any longer in constant fear by the haunting, even by its presence of the skull decided to challenge both the legend and the skull itself, obtaining church permission to have Roger Downes' coffin opened to see if his skeleton was headless. It was not. To whom then did the skull belong? Thus yet another version of the legend was born, equally unauthenticated.

This time it was established that the head belonged to a Roman Catholic priest named Barlow, known by everyone as 'Father Ambrose'. He was the son of Sir Alexander Barlow of Barlow Hall, which was near Wardley Hall. Wardley Hall was then occupied by John and Francis Downes, close friends of the Barlows. All were Roman Catholics and because of intense religious persecution frequent secret Masses were held in both Halls. Father

Ambrose was finally caught holding one of his secret Masses and arrested in 1641, he was executed and his head impaled on the tower of Manchester Old Church. A devout sympathizer managed to secure the head and bring it secretly back to Wardley Hall.

As if these legends were not enough to lay the skull to its final place in ghost history, it became a national sensation when, in 1930, it was stolen from Wardley Hall. There was an invasion of photographers and journalists of almost all the national and local press. Naturally the skull and its history became 'exclusive' with headlines of local stories fed to them by the locals, in a welter of misinformation and nonsense. In 1931 the skull secretly arrived back at Wardley Hall from the frightened thieves who had been haunted by it almost at once and was once again restored to its recess at the head of the staircase. So, after nearly four centuries the mystery remains unsolved, which might at least prevent the appearance of yet another legend.

When I had finished the story of Wardley Hall I received from Manchester County Libraries a message informing me that the Bishop of Salford is now the official resident of the Hall and giving me his telephone number. I rang his secretary about the skull, asking if it would continue to stay there. He informed me that of course it would. I then asked him if I could end my story expressing a hope that the Bishop would bring peace at last to both the skull and the Hall, and he said with a laugh, 'Certainly, the Bishop would enjoy that!'

Lancashire: *The Woman Embalmed in Tar: Birchen Bower*

When the *Manchester Guardian* of 22 July 1868 published news of the interment of a corpse embalmed in tar, which had been on view in the Manchester Museum for a century, the astonishing story of Miss Beswick became public. Since then it has been a widely-known North country legend and is still spoken about. It is no wonder that her ghost has been seen so many times and by so many people.

Miss Beswick lived in a quaint four-gabled manor house built in the form of a cross at Birchen Bower, Hollinwood, near Manchester. It was beautifully situated, surrounded by woods, fields, and farmlands. Her estates also included Rose Hill and Cheetwood. Most of the house was demolished after her death, except for the southern wing and a large barn bearing the date 1728. The latter was still standing in the early part of this century and is the source of all the legends about her hauntings.

She apparently farmed her own land, was very eccentric, and, when she became too old to manage the house and farm, she moved into a little stone cottage near to the manor house, which stood on the banks of a mill stream which rippled through her estates. Two very important things happened which changed the whole course of her life and finally led to her embalmed body lying for so long in the room of the Manchester Natural History Society. It might be there even now had the Commissioners not decided to have it interred 'deeming the specimen undesirable'.

Her first great shock came when news of the Jacobite Rebellion of 1745 brought Prince Charles, at the head of a Scottish army, sweeping south where, almost unopposed, he was already in the neighbourhood of Manchester. As she was, local legend claims, a very wealthy woman she at once, like so many others, hid all that she could somewhere on her estates, the whereabouts known only to herself. As it happened the rebels never reached her lands, and for a number of years Miss Beswick lived in peace once more, though not disturbing her secret hiding place or divulging to anyone the whereabouts of 'the vast sums of money and articles of value' she had reputedly hidden.

Her second shock was much greater. It was when her brother died, or so she and everyone else thought, including even the doctor who had been attending him through his illness. Her brother was actually in his coffin and the lid about to be screwed down when to her horror she saw that he was showing signs of life. She immediately stopped the undertaker and had her brother taken back to his bed. There he lay in a coma for some days, he recovered and lived for many years after his grim experience.

The possibility of being buried alive made a vivid impression on Miss Beswick. There and then she drew up a Will with her solicitor, as strange a document as any devised by law before or since. At the time the family doctor was Dr White to whom and his descendants she left all her estate. They were to receive the gross income from all sources 'as long as her body was kept above ground'. She further stipulated that at the end of every twenty-first year her body was to be sent to her old home at Birchen Bower and left there for a whole week. Shortly before her death she told relatives that if they would carry her from her cottage to the manor house she would show them where her treasure was buried. She was very insistent about this, but nothing was done on the day she made her request to them. She then became too ill to be moved at all, and died a few days later.

After her death Dr White had her body swathed in bandages, except for the face which was exposed, and embalmed in tar, and presented the corpse to the Natural History Society. He then settled down to enjoy the income now legally his and which was evidently going to be so for a very long time.

That the transport of her body to Birchen Bower was effectively carried out every twenty-first year after her death was vouched for by villagers in the year 1888 when, said the older folks, it had been there five times. They said it was always put in the granary of the old farmstead. Legend states that on the morning the corpse was to be brought there the horses and cows were always found loose, and sometimes a cow would be found up in the hayloft. According to Mr Ingram who made a close personal investigation into the whole strange case of Miss Beswick, there was no evidence of the truth of this. Nevertheless, the villagers firmly believed it was all the work of the supernatural. Indeed, Mr Ingram says, he met men who swore they had helped the cow down from the hayloft with ropes and tackle.

If, however, none of these things were true it was very certain to everyone that the ghost of Miss Beswick haunted the granary throughout the week her corpse lay there and even after it had been taken away again.

After Miss Beswick's death the manor house was divided into several separate dwellings, and it was there that her ghost became a familiar sight, though it never caused alarm. Several villagers saw her, usually as they were seated at table having supper. They would first hear the rustling of her silken dress and then see her enter the house, dressed all in black, gliding straight through the kitchen into the parlour, where she would always vanish at one particular flagstone.

'It was,' says John Ingram, 'a harmless spirit, annoying no one, and its appearance never drew forth any further remarks than "Hush! The old lady comes again." ' One of the villagers had a treadle-lathe for wood turning which he would use in the evening after his day's work. Often when he went into his room an invisible figure would be working the lathe in full motion.

These were the terrible years known as the 'Barley Times' which hit hard at poor people, for flour rose to a record price so that they could not afford to buy bread. Almost everybody in the district were loom weavers and near starvation, except for one of their number known to them all locally as 'Joe at Tanner's'. Everyone was puzzled at the amount of money he was spending, since times were so hard and wages at rock bottom. Joe had a large family, which made it all the more mysterious, since he earned the same wages as all the other men; yet he stinted nothing for his wife and many children.

As he lived in one wing of Birchen Bower, rumours and whispers began to circulate, for everyone for miles around knew only too well the story of Miss Beswick's hidden treasure. But there was never any proof that he had found it, only rumours and speculation, and no one dared accuse him of theft. What had been seen by some of them, however, was proof positive that something peculiar was going on. Joe was once seen carrying a heavy tin box to Oliphants, Goldsmiths and Jewellers, in St Anne's Square, Manchester. When he came out he was smiling very broadly and obviously well satisfied. From that time his standard of living began to rise, and in contrast with the poverty surrounding him he was very prosperous indeed. He continued so for a number of years before eventually confessing what had happened. One day, he said, he decided to fit up a loom on which to teach his children to weave. When he had pulled up the floorboards he discovered a large tin box full of wedges of solid gold. He took these to Oliphants, who paid him £3. 10/- a wedge, a great deal of money in those days. The tin box was said to have been handed down to his descendants as a family heirloom.

Legend had always said that once the treasure had been found Miss Beswick's ghost would be laid and her spirit cease to haunt her old home, but this was not so at all. She was seen as recently as 1920 near the old well by her former stone cottage, at a time when a presumed heir was pressing his claim to her estates. A villager going to draw water saw a lady standing there and said, 'She was dressed in a black silk dress and a white cap with a frilled border of stiff, old-fashioned puffs formerly worn by her.' It was dusk and she stood by the well in a hostile, even threatening, attitude. Ingram again writes: 'A stream of blue light seemed to dart from her eyes and flash on the terror-stricken man. This appearance of the lady's apparition was considered as a token that she would get no rest until the estates had reverted to the true heir.'

It would seem that the true heir never did turn up, for her spirit still haunts what little is left of her estates, swallowed up as they are in the straggling suburbs of Manchester. On dark and stormy nights the barn is said to appear to be on fire, glowing through the cracks and loopholes in its structure. So unearthly are the noises coming from it at such times that few, if any, will dare go near it, or knock up the farmer to tell him his barn is on fire. Whenever the barn is searched, however, there are no signs of charred wood anywhere, but legend is certain that somewhere near there the bulk of the treasure was hidden. The ghost was often seen going from the barn to the horsepool and vanishing and many people believed the treasure had been buried there, but no one ever substantiated their theories by investigation. Her body at least is at peace, for when it was removed from the Manchester Museum it was interred in Harpurhey Cemetery, which does not seem to be too unreasonable after lying embalmed in tar for one hundred years. It would, presumably, be wrong to suppose that the doctor, who enjoyed her income for so many years, might also have known where the treasure had been hidden and enjoyed that as well. But there was never any proof of that, thus adding still more to the mystery of the strange case of Miss Beswick of Birchen Bower.

Northumbria: The Relentless Poltergeists of Willington Mill

It is doubtful if any ghost story in the history of the occult has been more documented and authenticated than that of Willington Mill, formerly in Tyneside and now in Northumbria. The owner, Mr Joseph Procter, kept a meticulous diary of events for the first seven years of his tenancy before the relentless, merciless poltergeists finally drove him out five years later. It is quite incredible that anyone could have endured such torments for twelve terrifying years.

Procter was an 'elder' of the Society of Friends, a man of outstanding integrity and truth. So great was the value of his diary that, forty years after his death, his son Edmund was persuaded to hand it over to the Psychical Research Society for publication in their invaluable Journal.

The three-storeyed house with its contiguous mill was built about 1800 and almost at once, without any apparent reason, it gained a sinister reputation. It was first occupied by Joseph's cousin named Unthank, also a Quaker and both of them partners in their own firm Unthank & Procter. During Unthank's tenancy of twenty-five years, though warned that one room was supposed to be haunted, he had no trouble at all with ghosts. His family moved into the dwelling-house, but put one of the employees, Thomas Mann and his wife, into the mill, he to be clerk and foreman. The top part of the house was totally empty and unfurnished, with some of the windows bricked up and others firmly bolted; they were never occupied at all. Yet it was from a room in this part of the house that most of the noises later came when Joseph Procter and his family took over the premises. Thumps, knockings, heavy tramping of boots up and down on the wooden floor, slamming of doors and heavy cases being pushed across the floor echoed through the house night and day, from the very beginning of the Procters moving in.

The family, nurse and staff of maids occupied the dwelling house on 28 January 1835, retaining Thomas Mann as foreman of the flour mill. Only six weeks later Joseph entered the first account in his diary of the disturbances which, though fortunately he did not know it, were finally to drive them all out. It records the fear and alarm of the children's nurse who had put up with a number of mysterious and frightening noises for nearly two months not daring to tell either her master or mistress, until finally she could stand it no longer. She told Mr Procter she could no longer stay in the house for neither she nor the child were able to sleep for the noise of heavy tramping feet above her, the crashing movements of heavy cases or furniture being dragged across the uncarpeted wooden floor and her utter exhaustion caused by these noises.

She stayed a few days longer and left when a new nurse had been engaged, but the staff were strictly forbidden to disclose to the newcomer what strange things had taken place. The second nurse had not been there very long before she, too, became frightened at the same noises. On telling the other maids and being told by them of what they knew only too well but were forbidden to speak about, she went at once to Mr Procter, who seeing 'that it quite overset her', at once ordered a thorough search of both the nursery and the top floor, but nothing was found that could substantiate the constant reports of the disturbances.

During the next few days, no fewer than six different people were guests of the Procters all of whom heard disturbing noises 'and all were confident that the worst noises came from the unoccupied top room.' The next alarm came on 31 January at 1 a.m. from outside the house, in the yard between it and the mill. The mill foreman, Thomas Mann was on duty until 2 a.m. He had gone into the yard to fetch some coal, but was suddenly disturbed by a loud clanking noise, caused by what seemed to be something very heavy on iron wheels bumping up and down on the cobblestones of the yard. He could see nothing, but on his return with the coal he noticed that the wooden cistern on iron wheels which Mann used to water the horses was the obvious source of the noise that had mystified him. However, it had not moved from its accustomed place for there were no wheel-marks and no water in the cistern, just as he had left it.

That same night the Procters were kept awake in their bed 'by ten or twelve obtuse deadened beats of a mallet on a block of wood'. Drawing aside the bed curtains they saw the crib only two feet away, but the child slept peacefully. Then 'I heard a tap on the cradle leg as if with a piece of steel . . . ', but it did not wake the child. During the next few days there were fresh noises, a handbell was rung, the slow winding of a grandfather clock which only Mr Procter could hear, and always, day and night, the stamping of feet and the movement of heavy cases from the top floor.

The strangest event of all was the second mystery which took place outside the house. A neighbour told Mr Procter that she had clearly seen the apparition of a white figure in one of the second-storey windows. This was followed by Mr and Mrs Mann, whilst crossing the mill yard two nights later suddenly seeing in one of their windows the luminous and transparent figure of a woman. Struck with terror they saw the figure slowly sinking downwards until it disappeared. It took some ten minutes before the figure finally vanished.

Incident followed incident so quickly that one really wonders how Procter could record it all. Nurse Pollard complained of being lifted up in her bed at night as if there were a man under it. The child had cried out for some light and both of them were terrified and wanted to change the nursery. Doors were banged in locked rooms, windows were heard opening and slamming shut, and always there was the heavy stamping of boots thumping up and down in the top room. Perhaps one of the nastiest experiences was for Mrs Procter who, her son Edmund remembers, told him the story twenty or thirty times 'feeling very sick each time she did so.' One night she was awakened by a powerful force on her closed eyes like ice-cold fingers pressing her eyeballs in and terrifying her more than anything she could remember.

Later on, the children were playing together when one cried out that a monkey was pulling at his leg. All the others gathered round and scrambled under the bed to find the animal, but there was nothing there. Yet the child who had been attacked had no doubt at all that he had seen a monkey. One of the others then said that he had seen a white cat the day before, but no cat was ever in the house. The most extraordinary white cat with a pointed nose was actually seen by Mr Procter himself as it jumped into the engine-house in the mill and disappeared in the fireplace.

Then the most extraordinary event of all happened, one which finally decided the Procters to do something to prove these phantoms and noises were real. By now the village was full of gossip and rumours about them all. Mr Procter, therefore, invited two outside witnesses to come and sit up with him one night and, without any knowledge of what had been happening for so many years, a certain Dr Drury and a Mr Hudson agreed to come and sit up all night with him. The family had been sent away, probably quite willingly, and only Mr Procter and his manservant Bell were left with the two invited guests. They began a rigorous search of all the rooms in the house, the engine-room and the flour mill before they all settled down for the night. They did not have to wait very long, for as Mr Procter recorded:

About one o'clock I heard a most horrid shriek from E.D., slipped on my trousers and went up. He had then swooned, but come to himself again in a state of *extreme nervous excitement*, and accompanied with much coldness and faintness. He had seen the G.; had been struck speechless as it advanced from the closet in the room over the drawing-room to the landing, and then leapt up with an awful shriek and fainted.

Dr Drury later wrote a long letter to Mr Procter in which he certified what he had seen. He had taken out his watch to see the time, 'In taking my eyes from the watch they became rivetted upon a closet door, which I distinctly saw open, and saw also the figure of a female attired in greyish garments, with the head inclining downwards, and one hand pressed upon the chest, as if in pain, and the other viz., the right hand, extended towards the floor, with the index finger pointing downwards.'

Dr Drury goes on to relate how the ghost advanced towards Mr Hudson who was sleeping in his chair. As she walked fast towards the sleeping figure, Dr Drury rose from his chair and rushed at her to prevent whatever she meant to do. He made a swift move to seize her, but his outstretched arms encircled only air. Unable to save himself he fell upon the sleeping Mr Hudson and giving the piercing scream which Mr Procter heard fainted, as both fell to the floor. It was a long time before Dr Drury recovered from the very great shock he had received.

It was enough for the Procters, more than enough indeed for anyone. In 1847, after twelve long years of accumulative torture by spirits, the dreaded poltergeists, and their unending attacks, the family decided to move to live in North Shields, where surely such happenings could not be made upon them in a new house, where there were entirely new villagers. Their last night at Willington Mill was the most fiendish of them all. It was a merciless and concentrated attack by their enemies, as they had now become, convinced as they were that to struggle on against them was impossible, the Procters were worn out and totally powerless to deal with whoever these invaders were. All the many noises, footsteps, thumps, bangs, slamming of doors and moving of furniture they had endured was magnified into a colossal outburst of unimaginable terror and noise, as if the poltergeists themselves were arranging the removal and shifting all the furniture.

The family went to live in Camp Villa, North Shields, and were never again molested by phantoms or any noises, but lived quietly and at peace until Mr Procter's death. After their departure from Willington Mill, the dwelling-house was divided into two separate ones. The mill continued under the care of Thomas Mann until that, too, was sold to a firm of guano merchants from Newcastle, whose premises had been burnt down. Mr Procter never communicated with anyone at his former house or with the village people, but his son records that there were frequent mysterious disturbances which forced two tenants to leave.

The mystery of the persecution carried out at Willington Mill will never be solved. Indeed, if Mr Procter had not kept such a detailed record of the events there, nothing would ever have been known about the poltergeists. It is a great credit to the Society for Psychical Research that they published it in their Journal for posterity and most especially for those interested in the occult.

Yorkshire: The Gruesome Ghost of Calverley Hall

The legend of Walter Calverley is unquestionably the most gruesome in Yorkshire folklore, or for that matter in any other county. Though the Calverley family date back as far as the reign of King Stephen in 1135, when they first lived in Calverley Hall in the village of their own name, strangely enough Walter is the only notorious member of the family. That is simply because of the double murder of two of his three children, attempted murder of his wife, and thwarted murder of his third child, his terrible sentence of death by 'pressing' and his grim hauntings.

His marriage was at first quite happy, but the decline began when he tired of the life of the country squire and went to London, only returning home at short intervals. In the capital he led a life of unlimited pleasure, wenching, dicing, gambling, squandering his money in all directions and drinking heavily. It did not take many years for him to become on the verge of bankruptcy, mortgaging the ancestral home, forcing his wife to give up her dowry to pay his debts and finally repudiating a bond for £1000 for which his brother had acted as guarantor and was imprisoned for non-payment of the debt. It was then that he returned to the Hall and for some inexplicable reason suspected his wife of being unfaithful. In a fit of delirium tremens, according to one narrator, he went berserk with jealousy and hate, and on 23 April 1604, he burst into the Hall rushing up the stairs where his four-year-old son was standing. In a blind fit of rage which must have terrified the child, he drew his dagger and drove it into his son's head, carrying the bleeding child into the bedroom where his wife lay asleep.

The nurse, with the second child in her arms, rose in alarm and terror from her seat by the fire as Walter snatched the boy from her arms, driving his dagger into its body whilst still holding the first dead body under one arm. Then, as he dropped both the corpses to the floor, he seized the nurse, dragged her screaming to the door and flung her headlong down the steep flight of stone stairs, before turning and driving his dagger into his wife's body as she attempted to rise from her bed, awakened by the terrible noise. As she fell to the floor by her two dead sons, Walter sure that she too was dead, dashed downstairs, beating aside the staff gathered round the inert body of the nurse, fought off one of the male staff and rushed out to the stables, where he mounted one of his swiftest horses, galloping off towards Norton to murder his third son who was in that village with his nurse.

By then the hue and cry had been raised and local riders were in hot pursuit. Walter had arrived 'within a bow-shot of the house where his son lay' when his horse stumbled and fell, throwing Walter to the ground, where he was shortly arrested and taken to the nearest magistrate, who ordered him to be sent to Wakefield Gaol, not to York, because the plague was then raging in the city. Four months later he was taken to York Assizes and there tried for murder. By now he had recovered his reason sufficiently to refuse to plead guilty and was sentenced to the cruel and lingering death known in those times as *peine forte et dure*, which meant being crucified on a stone floor with heavy weights on the abdomen, gradually increased in weight until the victim was crushed to death. Many criminals, especially the richer ones, underwent the torture for the sake of their families, for it meant their property would not pass to the Crown, whereas had they pleaded and been found guilty, their property would by law, have passed to the Crown in forfeit.

Tradition says the torture was carried out in York Castle and that when one of his retainers visited him and removed some of the weights to relieve the agony of his master, he was executed for his action. Tradition also has it that Walter was buried in St Mary's Church in Castlegate, York, but that his body was later secretly disinterred and reburied in Calverley churchyard, where many of his ancestors were buried. The Calverley church register makes no mention of this but has recorded '1605 April William and Walter, sonnes of Walter Calverley Esqr. buried ye xx1111 day'. Whether his skeleton lies there or not, his spirit was not peaceful enough to stop him haunting the churchyard whereas he did not haunt St Mary's Church in Castlegate, York.

Walter Calverley's ghost began its haunting shortly after his death, terrorizing the local people. It had already been sought out by journalists for all the gory details of his murders and his death. The most haunted place was the lane leading from the Hall to Calverley church. The apparition always took a cloud-like, vaporous form of a figure with an angry face and mad eyes, holding in its hand a bloodstained dagger. Those unfortunate enough to see it said the figure came rushing at one in a fast gliding movement before disappearing in a vaporous mist and vanishing.

Even worse are the apparitions of Calverley and some of his drunken cronies dashing from the woods on headless horses as they shout out, 'A pund o' more weight. Lig on! Lig on!' in the Yorkshire dialect for death by 'pressing'. At other times he alone, or the group of headless horses would be seen rushing into the village or out to the Hall, where they would dash about the grounds and through the door into the Hall itself, then up the stairs into the room where the murders took place. Even worse are the ghosts of the two little murdered children, weeping bitterly and crying out for their mother.

One account of the sighting of the Calverley ghost ends with these words: 'To all those readers who disbelieve this narrative I would ask them to walk down Calverley Cutting by night, and if by the time they arrive at the bottom they are not willing to believe in something supernatural then I say they are made of sterner stuff than most people'. The Vicar of Calverley attempted an exorcism 'for so long as the hollies grow green in Calverley Wood', but without much success in 'laying his ghost'.

There was certainly intermittent peace for some time but the hauntings came to life strongly again towards the end of the eighteenth century, when Mr Burdsall, a Wesleyan preacher invited to Calverley to preach on the Sunday, was given hospitality at the Hall on Saturday night. He was shown into a large oak-panelled bedroom and after saying his prayers he settled down to sleep. He has left a true and detailed account of that night without, as he himself avers, any previous knowledge at all of what had happened almost two centuries before:

I had not been asleep long before I thought something crept up to my breast, pressing me much. I was greatly agitated and struggled hard to awake. The bed seemed to swing as if it had been slung in slings and I was thrown to the floor . . . I was thrown out a second time and going back once more I was thrown out a third time . . . I then crept under the bed and examined the cords which were fast. This was about one o'clock. I now put on my clothes not attempting to lie down any more.

As late as 5 January 1884, the *Yorkshireman* reported that thirteen years before, at one o'clock in the morning, Calverley church bell began to toll. It went on for some time while the villagers searched for the key, but when they had found the key and inserted it into the door the tolling ceased. Without making any attempt to find out if the bellringer was inside, or anyone was playing a prank, everyone there and in the village was absolutely convinced that it was Walter Calverley's ghost.

Shortly after that the village boys carried out a very strange ritual in an effort to 'raise' Walter Calverley's ghost once again, as if through the centuries the Yorkshire people had not been sufficiently terrified. They would meet near the church, place their caps in a pyramid, mingle pins and breadcrumbs together and dance heavily and slowly round and round, singing:

> Old Calverley, Old Calverley, I have thee by the ears.
> I'll cut thee into collops unless thee appears.

Some of the boys were then detailed to whistle through the church keyhole and repeat the rhyme, waiting to see if old Calverley's ghost would appear. According to the writer of this story, who, as a boy took part in the ceremony, 'something' did appear and the terrified boys fled in all directions, sure it really was the ghost they had challenged to appear. Perhaps one day it will appear again, but since that time there have been no reports of the gruesome murderer dashing through the village on a headless horse.

5 The South East

Hampshire: The White Garter Ghosts at Portsmouth

It was well after midnight in the early 1790s when Mr Samwell, an officer in the Royal Navy, at last saw the flickering light of an inn ahead of him outside the city of Portsmouth. Hastening his steps, he reached the heavy dark door, above which swung a signboard with the words 'White Garter Hotel' on it. For over an hour he had tramped the city to find a room but every inn, hotel and tavern was closed or full up. The coach on which he had travelled had been delayed by a wheel accident and he had missed his appointment at the Naval Dockyard.

He knocked hard a second time on the door and at last heard footsteps on the stone floor. The door was heavily and noisily unbolted and unchained, revealing a figure holding it half-opened. She was young, reasonably well dressed, with dark gypsy-like features and hard, repellent eyes, not unlike those of a snake. She stood silently, her eyes watching him with suspicion. He asked if he could have a room and breakfast. She still said nothing so he repeated his request. She said there was only one room available with two beds, one of which any late arrival would occupy. He said he did not want strangers and would pay for the second bed.

Only then did she let him in and picking up a rush-candle led him along the stone passage to the wooden staircase. Within seconds he felt there was something sinister about the place; the landlady, for she was surely that; the dark furniture; the staircase with the flickering light from the rush-candle causing shadows to leap about

101

on the walls and ceiling. They reached the room on the first floor; without a word she beckoned him in, closed the door and went downstairs again. He had not even moved before she returned to hand him a lighted candle and a heavy iron key. The oppression of the whole room gave him the feeling of a gathering storm. It was full of heavy locked oak cupboards, recesses and a window he could not open. It was also very cold. Too tired to worry any more, but very uneasy, he undressed and in spite of the coarse cold sheets, was soon asleep.

Samwell had no idea how long he had slept but suddenly something struck terror into him. In the flickering light of the guttering rush-candle, he saw with horror a figure approaching the foot of the bed. Propping himself upright, Samwell watched the figure dumbfoundedly. It was that of a heavily-built man dressed in a shaggy coat, a slouched black hat pulled down almost over his eyes and holding above his head a large lantern. As the figure raised his free arm he closed his fist as if to strike Samwell, who suddenly leapt out of the bed and hit out at the intruder, wincing with pain as his closed fists hit the wall behind the figure that had vanished. All his early fears and suspicions were confirmed and hastily dressing he moved to the door which was safely locked from the inside and crept noiselessly down the stairs to the front door, cautiously drew back the heavy bolt, released the chain, half-opening the door as a safeguard as he shouted aloud for the landlady. Almost at once she was at the head of the stairs, a lighted candle held above her head, behind her a most evil-looking man.

'Here's your money,' shouted Samwell, throwing it on the floor, 'I'm not staying here a minute more.' With a swift movement he was out into the darkened lane and running fast, though no one followed. Stumbling and falling in the rutted lane, with no sense of direction at all, he somehow reached the seafront and more light, determined to report his experience to some authority in the morning. As dawn broke he met a constable who told him that there were constant complaints about the place, its strange lights and phantom figures. It would be best, he said, to see the Mayor, Sir John Carter, who was not slow in acting for on his next visit to Portsmouth, Samwell heard that the inn had been demolished, the landlord and his wife arrested, and skeletons of murdered bodies excavated in the garden.

Many, many years had passed before a Mr Harrison, curiously enough also a naval officer, summoned from London to report the next day to the Naval Dockyard, had the usual difficulty in finding a room for the night, but at last found one called the White Garter Hotel. It seemed comfortable enough and without any knowledge of what had happened before he took a room, paying for both beds to avoid a stranger sharing the room. He settled down and wrote a few letters before he undressed, then he securely locked the door, bolted the window and went to sleep in one of the beds.

Something inexplicable woke him and in the moonlight that penetrated the room he saw by his watch that it was two o'clock. He was just about to duck under the bed-clothes again when, to his anger, he saw that the second bed was occupied. Furious that the landlady had let some-one else in with her duplicate key, he decided he would get up and complain at once and have a constable called to deal with the stranger. Then he noticed that the figure was quite still and made no noise at all. It could have been that of a sailor as the body was only partially dressed in trousers and a vest and was sprawling on the bed fast asleep. The moon no longer shone into the room so Harrison could not see the head. Having made up his mind to leave it until the morning, Harrison turned over and was soon asleep again.

When next he awakened, the room was in broad daylight and remembering he had an appointment he sprang out of bed. In a flash and struck motionless with shock and terror he saw the figure in the next bed. The face was heavily whiskered and as black as the thick curly hair just visible under the blood-soaked bandage wrapped over the head and face. In a fraction of time, Harrison was out of the room and down the stairs, where he almost knocked over the landlady who gazed at him in astonishment, before asking what was the matter.

'The matter?' gasped Harrison. 'Do you mean that you don't know there's another man in the room with something seriously wrong with him? Here, take the money, I'm not staying here another minute.' He pushed the money into her shaking hand as she stammered out, 'I don't understand what you are talking about. No one came to the hotel after you. No one. You must be dreaming.' Then, as he made a swift move to leave, she suddenly halted him by her next remark. He turned to see her body trembling, her face salt-white, her frightened eyes staring as she whispered the words. 'You must have seen "Whiskers', sir. I feared he would never rest.'

'What on earth are you babbling about?' asked Harrison furiously, more anxious than ever to go.

'Did he have black hair and black whiskers?' she persisted, 'Was he dressed like a sailor?'

'I don't know, he only had trousers and a vest on and a blood-soaked bandage over his head and I'm now going to report it to the police.'

'It was "Whiskers" you saw. It was his ghost. I knew he would come back. I knew it. I must tell someone. I can't go on keeping it to myself.'

She then told him the whole story:

A party of sailors arrived one night recently and were drinking very heavily in the bar but two of them took their bottles up to the room where you slept last night, to play cards, which they did until the other one swore that "Whiskers" had cheated. There was a row, a fight started and "Whiskers" was struck over the head by a heavy glass bottle and was dead almost at once. The sailor was in a terrible panic. He said he would be sent to prison for murder and probably hanged and would I let him be buried in the garden. I could do nothing but give in. Then some of the other sailors helped to get the body down and bury it in the garden where it is still. It was his ghost you saw. I knew it. Please say nothing.

Harrison without another word left the hotel to keep his appointment only to be informed that he had been posted to the Colonies and would be leaving shortly. There was no time to report to the authorities and he would have to keep the secret alone. It was fifteen years before he returned to England. Out of sheer curiosity he decided to find out if the White Garter Hotel was still there, but everything had changed and he was not even sure where it had been.

The strange thing about these two stories is that the White Garter Hotel has been demolished three times. Each time skeletons have been discovered in the garden. A new block of buildings has now been erected on the site, and one wonders if "Whiskers" and other ghosts still haunt the place.

Kent: *The Earthbound Children of Ramhurst Manor*

The story of the ghostly couple haunting the early eighteenth-century Ramhurst Manor House, still shown on the Ordnance Survey map, near Tonbridge in Kent, was considered by experts in the supernatural at the time to be one of the most mysterious ever recorded. The principal investigator was Robert Dale Owen, who, in his book *Footfalls on the Boundary of Another World*, published in 1878, wrote a full account of it.

As so often happened in the early nineteenth century the surnames of people in the book were represented by the initial letter and a dash, which not only seems to make the whole narrative less convincing but is always tedious. As this is the only authentic version, however, it has to be endured.

Ramhurst Manor, situated on the River Medway near Leigh and Tonbridge, was occupied in October 1857 by a Mrs R—, wife of a high-ranking British officer serving in India. From almost the very moment she and her staff of servants moved in the hauntings began. Their nights were made miserable by continuous knockings on doors and walls, unaccountable voices, often coming from empty rooms, and the sound of mysterious footsteps along the passages. Sometimes two voices could be heard, as if a conversation were going on. At other times, a single voice seemed to be reading aloud or a monk could be heard telling his beads. Once or twice an isolated, angry, and very loud voice was heard shouting orders or rebukes to a servant. It was not long before the servants became frightened, one or two of them gave immediate notice, willing to sacrifice their wages rather than stay any longer in the house.

One day the cook, in great alarm, told her mistress she had heard a new and very disturbing sound. This was the rustling of a silk dress so near to her that the figure wearing it almost touched her, though she saw nobody. Her horror exceeded her fear to such a degree that her mistress decided to call in her own brother. She well knew he would scorn and scoff at the whole idea of ghosts but he might pacify the staff by his own attitude. He, like her husband, was an officer and a great man for the open air and all field sports.

His very first night in the Manor, however, was so disturbing that even he had to admit very strange things were happening in the house. The two voices he suddenly heard talking together, which had awakened him, went on for so long that he was sure his sister was having a long conversation with a lady friend staying in the house at the time. Twice he was absolutely certain he heard his sister's voice. He was about to get up when her voice rose to a piercing and blood-chilling scream which echoed throughout the house. He sprang from his bed, seized the gun he had brought with him, rushed out of the room along the passage, and without even knocking burst into his sister's room. He found her fast asleep, not even aware of his noisy entry or his presence in the room at all.

On their third Sunday there, when the disturbances seemed to be uncontrolled and continuous, Mrs R— drove over to meet a great friend of hers, a Miss S—, with whom she had corresponded about the events at Ramhurst. Her friend had agreed to come and stay for a few weeks to make her own personal investigations, since she was deeply interested in the supernatural and was herself a medium, having been psychic from childhood. She was met by her hostess at Tonbridge railway station and driven over to Ramhurst Manor, reaching it about four o'clock in the afternoon. As they arrived at the entrance, Miss S— saw an elderly couple standing there as if to welcome them. They were dressed in the costume of a much earlier period that not until later could she define exactly. Though she was not in any way disturbed, or even surprised, so accustomed had she been throughout her life to seeing ghosts, she felt her friend might become still more uneasy than she was already, so she decided not to tell her about the old couple.

During the next few days she saw them often, in various rooms, in the passages, in the grounds, but always and only in the daytime. Strangely enough there were now fewer night disturbances. The couple were always enveloped in a strange grey-coloured mist 'of a neutral tint'. Then one day as she met them in one of the rooms they actually spoke to her. They seemed to be a very sad couple, and when Miss S— asked them who they were and what was troubling them they said they were husband and wife, and that their name was Children. They told her also that they were very upset and sad about the house. During their lifetime, when they built it, they had done so with loving care, sparing neither money nor devotion to make it beautiful. It had been their whole life, pride and joy, and would, they felt and intended, go on giving equal pleasure to their descendants. But this had not been fulfilled, for after they had died the property had deteriorated to its present state, which gave them only great sorrow. Then, as suddenly as they had appeared, the quiet old couple vanished.

Once again Miss S— decided to keep the whole strange encounter and conversation to herself. She casually asked her friend if she had ever heard of a family with the strange name of Children who might once have lived in the house. But Mrs R— said she had never heard of the name. In fact she did not know anything at all about the house and was not particularly interested in it since she and her family were only tenants until she returned to India to join her husband.

Miss S— began to make local enquiries, but no one had ever heard of anyone with that name living in the district, let alone the house. At night the disturbances, though less, still continued, with knockings, footsteps and voices but whereas the latter were wholly unintelligible to the rest of the household, to Miss S— they were clear enough for her to understand what they were saying. She became engrossed in the events taking place in the house, though Mrs R— , believing her to be as uneasy and fearful as she was herself, one day asked her if she wanted to go back home. Only then did Miss S— tell her all the details, and most especially of her conversation with the old ghostly couple who had given her their names and the reason for their sorrow. Until then only she had seen the ghosts, though everyone else in the house had heard them, but within the month Mrs R— herself saw them for the first time, and in a much more alarming and dramatic way.

Her brother, who in spite of his uneasy experience had continued to stay in the Manor, had been out shooting all day. Mrs R— was upstairs dressing for dinner when she heard her brother shouting up to her that he was famished, that dinner was being served, and it was about time she came down. A few minutes later he shouted up to her again, now angry and impatient at her delay. Nervously she hurried to finish her toilet and go down to him to keep the peace, his short temper being proverbial.

As she opened the door she saw the old couple standing there. They were just as Miss S— had described them in every detail. She now saw for herself the costumes of an earlier age, the old point-lace collar on the woman's silk brocaded dress being most distinctive. The figure and costume of her husband standing quietly and courteously on her left was less distinct. They stood in absolute silence, but more astonishing and frightening than their figures was the phosphorescent light surrounding the old lady.

Within this light were the words 'Dame Children', and below, less clearly, more words saying that as all her hopes and fears had been entirely of this earth she and her husband were therefore earthbound.

Stunned and horror-stricken at what she saw, Mrs R— heard once more the angry bawling voice of her brother impatiently demanding if there was to be any dinner at all that day, and if she was ever coming down. She wanted to move, but the figures blocked her path. Suddenly her panic overcame her fear, and closing her eyes, she rushed right through them, down the stairs and into the dining-room where she collapsed, babbling out incoherent words that silenced even her angry brother. As she turned to Miss S— she said, 'Oh, my dear, I've walked through Mrs Children.' It was the first and last time she ever saw them, but from that very moment she made the servants keep a blazing fire in her room by day, and candles and lamps burning by night. She also made up her mind to leave the house as soon as she possibly could.

Miss S— continued to see the old couple and in one of her conversations with them she received from the old gentleman vital clues as to his identity. He told her his Christian name was Richard and that he had died in 1753. It was then that she realised the costumes the old couple always wore were of the very late Queen Anne or early Georgian period; 'she could not be sure which as the fashions in both were similar', she afterwards stated.

At this point she and Mrs R— decided to tell the servants more than they had done so far, since being of local origin they might have some clues, but nothing emerged until Sophie, the nurse, who was not local, said she would ask her sister-in-law whose family had lived in Kent for generations. Sophie was at once given permission to go and see her sister-in-law, who had moved out of the district, to find out all she could about Ramhurst Manor and its first occupants, Mr and Mrs Children. Sophie's relatives were living at Riverhead, near Sevenoaks, and many years earlier had been in service at Ramhurst Manor, and must surely be able to supply some information.

When Sophie returned from her visit she managed to clear up some part of the mystery. Her sister-in-law had once been a housemaid at Ramhurst, though not with a family named Children. She remembered, however, a very old man once telling her when she was a child that he had been employed to assist the keeper of hounds at the Manor House, which was then, he was quite sure, owned by a Mr Children. When Sophie told her mistress and Miss S— all that she had heard, it confirmed that such a family did once exist and live in the Manor.

It was in December 1858 that Robert Dale Owen first heard the whole story whilst staying with Mrs R— and Miss S— at Ramhurst for Christmas. He became so involved in the whole mystery that he decided there and then to investigate the history of the Manor personally. This he did as soon as he could, after thoroughly examining all the statements Sophie had made. He inspected the records and graveyards of the churches at Leigh and Tonbridge, but only discovered the slender clue that in the year 1718, thirty-five years earlier than the date given by the ghost to Miss S—, a George Children had left a weekly dole of bread to the poor. He then discovered that another George Children had died forty years earlier still. He had never lived at Ramhurst, but had a marble monument erected to his memory in Tonbridge church.

His next discovery was most important, for a neighbouring clergyman lent him a document containing the following extract from the Hasted Papers in the British Museum:

George Children . . . who was High Sheriff of Kent in 1698 died without issue in 1718 and by Will devised the bulk of his estate to Richard Children eldest son of his late uncle William Children of Hedcorn, and his heirs. This Richard Children settled himself at Ramhurst, in the Parish of Leigh, . . . he had issue four sons and two daughters . . .

The puzzle then began to be solved for Owen had now proved that this Richard was the ghost, that he had settled there in the early part of the reign of George I, thus accounting for the costume the elderly couple wore; but he still had no proof of the date of Richard's death, 1753, which the ghost himself had given to Miss S—.

Owen next met an antiquarian friend who suggested he should consult Hasted's *History of Kent*, published in 1778, in which he found the following:

> In the eastern part of the parish of Lyghe (now Leigh), near the river Medway, stands an ancient mansion called Ramhurst, once reputed a Manor in the reign of Edward I and held by the Culpeper family for several generations . . . It passed by sale through Dixon to Mr William Saxby who conveyed it by sale to Richard Children. Richard Children resided here, and died possessed of it in 1753, aged eighty-three years. He was succeeded in it by his eldest son John Children of Tonbridge . . .

This verification of a date first uttered by a ghost is truly astonishing, and may well be the only example of its kind in the many records of the supernatural world. It also proved that Richard Children was the only member of the family who lived and died at Ramhurst as Owen further discovered that members of the Children family had been settled in Leigh and Tonbridge for centuries, but that the wealthy George Children, though possessing Ramhurst, was living at Ferox Hall, Tonbridge. He was the senior partner of the Tonbridge Bank, which was bankrupted in 1816 and so forced him to sell all his properties. It was the purchaser of Ramhurst Manor who turned the splendid house into a farmhouse, and was thus the cause of the sorrow brought to the ghosts of Richard Children and his wife, who felt their splendid home had been desecrated. Owen visited it at the time he wrote his book and says: 'All the occupants assured me that nothing worse than rats or mice disturb it now.'

It is, therefore, not to be wondered why the old couple were so disturbed and so sad about the desecration of their once beautiful house, built with so much loving care. As a ghost story it is surely unique, since all the information leading to a solution of the mystery of Ramhurst came from the other world verbally, and only then to a sympathizer and one who understood what it was to be earthbound, as the words above Dame Children's head had clearly stated. Had Miss S— not been able to communicate with them, the hauntings might well have continued.

However it was, all the disturbances ceased from the moment Owen solved the whole puzzle and proved the truth of the old ghost's statement about his beloved home. The quiet old couple found rest and peace again, but not before Mrs R—, unable to continue living there any longer, had given up her tenancy and returned to India.

Long after that, however, local legend believed that the hauntings would return if by any chance the property were to come once more into the hands of a descendant of the Children family. The oddest thing of all in the whole strange story is that since the hauntings ceased the name of Children has reappeared in the district.

Sussex: *Six Restless Spirits: Brede Place*

It was Sir Edwin Lutyens, the distinguished architect, who said that of all the many haunted houses in Sussex, Brede Place was the most interesting. This imposing Tudor mansion has throughout its six centuries of occupation been full of 'presences'. Some of them are disturbing, sinister, comforting, but all of them are very real. There are the ghosts of a man, a woman, a beheaded man, a priest, a mysterious scent of violets, and Marthe.

The last, a Tudor maidservant, is the unhappiest ghost of all, believed in even today by people in the neighbourhood. She was caught stealing one day by the then lord of the manor, who with typical feudal barbarity, had her hanged from an ash tree in a dell or ghyll, at the top of a hill behind the present house. As the years passed 'her ghost constantly haunted the scene of her execution, the tree becoming so rotten and hollow that Captain Frewen, then owner of the house, used it as a place to burn his rubbish. For a long period he had felt Marthe's presence to such a degree that he never felt easy when nearing the tree and found it impossible to do any work in the surrounding nearby garden. So in 1910 he decided to burn down the tree and hope by doing so that the ghost of Marthe would cease to disturb him. This was precisely what happened to his great relief, for he was able from then on to work quite undisturbed there.

During the Second World War the British Army took over the house and, as so often happened, they were not too careful of their treatment of the place. Many officers, particularly Canadians, had unpleasant encounters with ghosts in various rooms and in the grounds. The most positive evidence of a 'presence' and witnessed by all who felt it, was the day Father John's ghost walked through a file of men assembled in one of the corridors.

Papers, books, shoes, documents, clothing, all had an unaccountable habit of moving or disappearing altogether. At the time the new word 'gremlin' was invented to cover just this particular type of thing, as well as describing any misfortune or disaster caused by it. Some of the missing articles were never found, others discovered in empty or disused rooms a considerable way from the parts occupied by the army.

Towards the middle of the fourteenth century, the manor of Brede was granted by Edward III to one of his soldiers, Sir Thomas atte Ford. He, with the help of some monks, built a fine house with stone brought over from Caen in Normandy. When it was complete Edward III, together with his queen, lunched there before embarking for France on a military expedition.

The fact that Sir Thomas was assisted by monks to build the house seems to confirm, as has been suggested, that the site was formerly a holy place. After his death his daughter Jane brought the whole estate as a dowry when she married into the family of Oxenbridge, who lived and remained there for about 225 years. One of that family built the customary chantry on to the south aisle of Brede church, known as the Oxenbridge Chantry. Here lies the giant effigy of Sir Goddard Oxenbridge, together with another member of the family.

The legend of 'the Giant', as he was called, brought only fear to Sussex, for it was said that he was impervious to death by steel, and fed upon newborn babies. As terror of 'the Giant' spread, the Sussex children banded together, succeeded in getting him drunk, and dragged his great body to a place called Groaning Bridge in Stubb Lane. There they sawed him up with a wooden saw, distributing some of the pieces in the grounds of the manor house. As one of the ghosts of Brede Place is that of a headless man it has always been assumed this was Sir Goddard himself, perhaps searching for his sawn-off head somewhere in the 400-odd acres of estate. In the eighteenth century the smugglers made full use of this horror story to keep people in at night whilst they brought up their contraband brandy kegs from Hastings, only eight miles away.

In 1575 Brede Place came into possession of the family of Frewen, and has remained in their hands ever since. Just before that, however, one of the last Oxenbridges modernized the great house to the then prevailing Elizabethan style. He first floored over the Great Hall, then built a staircase. It was the latter which caused the secularization of part of the former chapel since it was built over the shrine containing the holy relics and gave access to the priest's upper room, formerly reached only by a ladder. It was this desecration which undoubtedly caused the priest's ghost to haunt not only the chapel and its adjoining rooms but the great staircase. He is affectionately called 'Father John', and so powerful is his presence on that staircase between the hours of ten o'clock at night and dawn that few will dare to use it.

When Captain Frewen, encouraged by his success in laying the ghost of Marthe, attempted to do the same with Father John he not only failed to do so but was actually driven from the staircase by the power of his 'presence' and never attempted to do so again. During restorations in 1830 the bones of a priest were found underneath the original altar; he wore a gilt cross round his neck. So haunted was the priest's room that it had to be taken down and this final action on top of everything else could not have helped Father John to feel at peace in that part of the house.

The late Sir Winston Churchill, a cousin of Clare Frewen, whose aunt was Lady Randolph Churchill, was a frequent guest at the house. On one of his visits he planted a golden yew in the grounds. He was, however, totally impervious to the 'presences', sleeping soundly at all times, though he accepted the possibility of their existence.

Clare Frewen became Clare Sheridan, the well-known sculptress, returning often and for long periods to Brede Place after her husband had been killed in the trenches in the First World War. She brought also her son Richard and her daughter Margaret. Margaret at the age of three saw her first ghost at Frampton, the Sheridan home. It was of a little boy dressed in sailor clothes, a white suit and a round straw hat, who passed her in silence on the stairs one day. She did not know until much later that she had seen a ghost of great ill-omen, for one of the Frewen ancestors had been a midshipman who was drowned at sea. To see him at all meant that an heir would die. Very shortly after, in fact, a letter came to the house announcing the death of her father. It was an experience terrifying enough for a young child, but even more so when the full knowledge of what her experience had meant came to her in later life. In fact she has recorded in her book how frightened she always was at Brede, 'with its hideous atmosphere'. It brought even more terror to her when a sinister ghost she always seemed to meet in the porch, which others had also seen, confirmed all her fears of yet another warning ghost. One day shortly afterwards her grandfather collapsed in the porch and never recovered consciousness, so perhaps he too had seen it and knew its meaning.

But it was her mother Clare, the sculptress, who turned more and more towards the occult, especially after the tragic death of her son in 1936. This broke her heart and almost destroyed her. At Brede, in spite of all, and perhaps even because of all she knew about the hauntings there, she found the great solace and peace she so desperately needed. She let the manor house and built for herself a studio in the grounds. There, through the help and guidance of a medium, who was also a friend, she began to seek out and live with the ghosts. She was in constant communication with spirits in the other world and most of all her son. He had died of appendicitis in Algeria two months after his twenty-first birthday, when he had inherited the Frampton estates.

In her book *My Crowded Sanctuary*, Clare Sheridan records her experiences, factually, graphically, yet with calm assurance and conviction. Her first attack was upon what she considered to be an evil spirit, the poor Tudor housemaid who had been so brutally hanged by her master. Though her brother was himself convinced he had laid her ghost, he had only done so as far as it affected him. Near the dell where the crime took place was a cattle-gate across a private road through the estate. Other drivers beside herself who used the road had been afraid to open the gate after dark. To lay Marthe's ghost Clare Sheridan decided she would go out at night and talk to Marthe. This she did asking the ghost why she could not herself open the gate for her. Marthe replied, 'I wish I could', before she vanished. She called the gate Marthe's Gate from that time and strangely enough many people who would never have dared go near the gate in the dark did so now without fear.

Then Father John appeared to her, just as he had done to others in the past, but with so much kindness, care, comfort and solicitude that he became a friend. It was in his chapel and alone with him that she found the peace and harmony she so urgently needed. Her deep gratitude was expressed in a wooden Madonna which she so lovingly carved for the chapel and which is there today.

It was from one of the haunted rooms near this chapel that a guest came running one night, unable to stay there any longer, and leaving the first thing next morning, never to return. Other strange things were happening, door-latches being lifted, footsteps, unidentifiable but disturbing sounds. There were parts of the garden where no one would dare go, nor in the dungeons. One owner once emerged from the cellar white-faced and badly shaken but absolutely refusing to say what he had seen or felt. Above this cellar, and at the top of the stairs leading to it, was once a rug which was being moved with constant deliberation for no reason at all. When it was replaced by another rug it remained always in place. Once there appeared an evil spirit of a man, full of violence, who told Clare Sheridan he was an Oxenbridge who, centuries before, had been stabbed in his sleep by his jealous neighbour.

In 1947 the sculptress was forced to sell Brede. The man who bought it was killed in a car accident three years later. Only by chance did the house come back from the open market into the Frewen family once again. Suddenly there were fresh, hitherto unknown mysteries. The unmistakable scent of violets in a room, a photograph by an expert which revealed a headless man, a visitation by a woman in a large dress and a ruff round her neck. It is almost impossible to believe that anybody could continue to live in such a house yet throughout almost four centuries during which the Frewens have occupied Brede Place the ghosts have never taken it over in sufficient strength to drive their owners away.

Perhaps it is the dominating influence, gentleness, counsel and guidance of Father John who loves it so much that he will never leave it. As long as he is there, it seems, no real harm can come to Brede Place, so why should its owners feel any fear or anxiety? The answer was firmly given by the mother of the Captain Frewen who burned down the ash tree. She used to read downstairs far into the early hours before going up the stairs where Father John's presence was so powerful. She had done much to improve the house, and especially the chapel. 'But what about the ghosts?' she was often asked. 'Oh, I don't mind them,' she replied, 'they are all *friendly* to me.'

6 The South West

Avon: Bristol's House of Fear

Just over sixty years ago, the *Clifton Chronicle* published a strange and gruesome story of a haunted house in Bristol which finally caused the death of the owner. It was a fine house in Stoke Bishop near the Clifton Downs, one of the most fashionable residential parts of Bristol today. Many years before the time of the reported tragedy, however, the neighbourhood was almost uninhabited, for no motor traffic ran across the Downs and tram-lines were far off. 'People then used Pitch and Pay Lane and Mariner's Lane more than they do now and it was like living in the country', which was the reason why Mr C (the paper did not give names so that future buyers would not be deterred from taking the place), decided to live there with his housekeeper and daughter Dorothy.

He was an old man of seventy-five, his daughter just fourteen. His wife had died two years earlier and the present housekeeper, Miss B., then employed as a maid, had nursed her through a long illness. Mr C. had never really recovered from his wife's death and was content to let the housekeeper run the house and look after Dorothy, whom he loved very dearly. All three seemed to get on very well together. After about a year, Miss B. began to discuss the education of Dorothy with her father. As there were few boarding schools in Bristol then, she asked Mr C. to agree to her going away somewhere where there was a good school. Mr C. was averse to the idea since he felt he could not part with Dorothy and the subject was dropped.

It was, however, Dorothy herself who told her father she would like to go away as life was so dull in Stoke Bishop and she had no friends of her own age, ideas obviously

118

given to her by the housekeeper. This finally persuaded Mr C. to agree to her going to a school at Great Malvern which the housekeeper had heard was a very good one. Letters were written, arrangements made, everything managed by the housekeeper. It was agreed that Dorothy should leave early in the morning and in order not to disturb her father, she would say goodbye to him the previous night. It was late September, and was a sad parting for both knew they would not see each other before Christmas.

It was not long before Mr C. regretted what he had agreed to with his housekeeper. He missed his daughter greatly, he had made no local friends and life was very dull indeed. A maid had been engaged some time earlier but was away on holiday and as both the housekeeper and her employer disliked strangers, there was little company. When the maid returned, she complained to the housekeeper that once or twice she had heard someone walking about upstairs, but when she went up to look there was nobody. The housekeeper said it must have been the wind rustling the ivy on the wall, or a creaking door and nothing more was said.

Towards the end of October, Mr C. was delighted to have a letter from a very old friend who was coming to Bristol on business and asked if he might stay a couple of nights with him. Mr C. told his housekeeper to prepare Dorothy's room, which, as it faced south, would be warmer. He was surprised at her annoyance, though he said nothing. When the next morning the visitor was asked by the housekeeper if he had slept well he said he had not, because there had been a child in the room disturbing him. He asked if Dorothy was at home and was puzzled to hear she was not, but was persuaded by Miss B. not to mention anything to his host.

Shortly after this, another friend of Mr C., a widow, asked if she could stay two nights and slept in the same room. She, too, asked the housekeeper the next morning who was the fair-haired young girl who came into her room last night. 'I spoke to her,' she said, 'but she did not answer.' In spite of the housekeeper's assurance that she must have been dreaming for there was no child in the house, the lady told Mr C., who was visibly disturbed. Strangely enough, a third visitor asked to come to the house for two nights and the same instructions to prepare Dorothy's room were unwillingly carried out. The very next morning the lady apologized to her host but said she could not stay another night in his house. She told him she had had a very bad night; a girl with long plaited hair had entered her room and stood looking at her for a long time as she stood at the foot of the bed. Mr C., now deeply concerned, decided to spend the night in Dorothy's room himself.

He had not been asleep long before he was awakened by something sinister. His bed faced the dying fire but in the glow he saw a figure moving towards him and the bed. With a shock of fear and surprise he recognized Dorothy. She stood with her arms outstretched as if to embrace him, but as he spoke to her she vanished. The next morning, without mentioning his experience to Miss B., he ordered her to send a telegram to the school to ask if his daughter was well, remembering that there had been two letters which Miss B. had read to him, saying Dorothy was quite happy where she was. Miss B. offered to send off the telegram at once and left to do this, leaving a now very suspicious Mr C. No reply came from the school, and about tea-time the maid came to report that Miss B.'s room was in great disorder and all her personal papers, money and jewellery were missing.

By now Mr C. was convinced of the seriousness of the situation and at once he sent the maid to dispatch a second telegram to the school. In a very short time he had a telegram back from the headmistress, who informed him that there had never been a pupil by his name at the school. There had earlier been some correspondence about her coming, but nothing more had been heard from the writer. Mr C. went at once to the police, for in those days there was no telephone, and returned with a detective and a policeman. They at once began a thorough search of the house from top to bottom. It was only towards the end of their search that they removed the carpet in Dorothy's bedroom and saw at once that the floorboards had been at some time removed and clumsily replaced. When these were once again taken up, they saw in the aperture the body of the little murdered girl.

Medical evidence revealed that she had been drugged and murdered in her sleep. A wide-scale search was organized to find the criminal, but the housekeeper had completely vanished and all efforts to trace her whereabouts were fruitless. It was thought by the police that once she knew the widespread search for her was on she might have committed suicide, but she was never found. Papers discovered in her room suggested that her intention had been to persuade her master that his daughter had died at school, though how she could ever have convinced him about this is quite inconceivable. It is more likely that Miss B. would perhaps have thought she would inherit her master's money when he died without a wife or daughter.

The grim and sordid details of the whole story hastened Mr C.'s own death. The phantom was never again seen by him and no record exists of her apparition in the empty house. The paper ended its report by saying that new tenants had bought it and had seen nothing at all of Dorothy's sad ghost, even though they must have been aware of the story before purchase.

Avon: Ghosts Galore in Bath

If ghost statistics are correct, Bath is the second most haunted city in Great Britain. London, of course, is the most haunted. The ghosts are numerous and varied, including two duellists, a grey lady, a man in Regency clothes, another man dressed as a Quaker, a naval commander, a man in a black hat, poltergeists and, quite incredibly, a butterfly ghost. They have been sketched and photographed by different people who have compared findings and agreed similar results. They have been seen in daylight, in the Assembly Rooms, the Theatre Royal and the principal streets. Sounds of voices have been heard in a house in Gay Street where Dr Samuel Johnson 'took tea with Mrs Thrale', who lived there in the eighteenth century. The voices have often been heard in animated conversation, but they ceased whenever the door was opened.

In the magnificent Great Pulteney Street, where so many rich and well-known people lived, the house where Admiral Howe, who commanded the Channel Fleet in the French war of the eighteenth century, resided has been consistently haunted by his phantom in full naval uniform. The Grosvenor Hotel, once the home of the poet William Wordsworth, now a block of flats, has an ice-cold ghost of a vaporous lady who was once seen entering the Conference Room seating herself at the long table, though there was no sign of a chair having been moved nor any sound of footsteps. She has often been seen on the stairs and in the corridors.

York Villa, once the house of George III's second son the Duke of York, has long been haunted by an unhappy and miserable ghost, the Duke's retainer, an old and trusted servant. The Duke, whose scandalous and libidinous life was widely known, one day told his mistress, of whom he was tired, that he was going to London. She decided to follow him and left the old retainer to look after the two children. As the weeks passed and neither the Duke nor his mistress returned, the unpaid servants all decided to leave, including the old retainer. He, however, driven by his uneasy conscience, went back to see if the children were alive, only to find their bodies, for they had starved to death. His footsteps have often been heard up and down the stairs and wandering through the rooms.

One of the most frequently seen ghosts is called the Man in a Black Hat. No one has ever discovered who he was, where he lived, or what was his history, only that he haunts the Assembly Rooms and the streets. He wears a long black cloak and a large black hat and his appearances are documented as far back as 1711 when the Assembly Rooms were first built. No doubt he was one of the first men to frequent the place. He has been sketched, photographed, seen by daylight and at night, a solidly built figure moving quite fast and noiselessly. Of all the Bath ghosts he is certainly the most familiar.

But by far the most notable ghosts in Bath are those in the Theatre Royal, the Garrick's Head Hotel, and the now blocked-up passage connecting them. They have been written about over and over again but it would be impossible to omit them from a history of Bath, for they have become very real persons to those who have seen them, especially the Grey Lady, that mysterious, unknown and very mischievous apparition. Visitors have seen her both inside and outside the theatre, actors have seen her many times and had tricks played on them by her. She always occupies one of the boxes. Once, when the play had a grandfather clock as part of the décor in a drawing-room, it began to chime the hour as the actors were speaking. The audience, at first accepting the chimes as part of the play, sat in astonishment as the clock went on chiming, the actors stopped speaking, and the clock still went on chiming until the Grey Lady stopped it and vanished. As late as 1975 during a performance of *The Dame of Sark* in which Dame Anna Neagle was the star, she and all the actors saw the Grey Lady, not once but two or three times.

One of the rarest phantoms ever seen in Great Britain was a butterfly. In 1948, the Christmas pantomime included a butterfly ballet in which the dancers were dressed as tortoiseshell butterflies. To the astonishment of everyone in the theatre an actual living tortoiseshell butterfly was seen flying about. It is said that at every Christmas pantomime since, the butterfly ghost has been seen.

The ghosts of the Garrick's Head Hotel are notorious. In 1730 the building was the private house and gaming-house of the great Beau Nash, a secret passage joining it to the Theatre Royal as an escape route for the gamblers if the house were raided. At least three ghosts as well as poltergeists haunt the hotel. There are the sounds of clashing swords from duellists, crashes and noises from the rooms, voices and even articles being hurled about by unseen means.

Another far more sinister lady ghost haunts what is now the hotel bar, formerly one of the gaming-rooms. In about 1780, a quarrel had broken out between two of the gamblers, each of whom claimed the favours of a very pretty lady who was also in the room. Oaths and shouts broke out and swords were drawn. The lady, quite unaware of the cause of the quarrel, watched in horror when she saw that one of the duellists was her lover. She fled in terror up the stairs to her own room, only to hear a cry of victory from the one who now followed her upstairs to claim her, having killed her lover. She flung herself from the window to the courtyard below, and has haunted the Garrick's Head Hotel ever since. It was the last duel to be fought in Bath, where duelling had always been the only way of settling a dispute. From that time Beau Nash, virtual monarch of the city, strictly forbade duelling.

The main hauntings in the hotel became even more sinister when the poltergeists took over. A few years ago when the landlord went down to draw beer from the barrels in the cellar, he smelt a very heavy perfume and felt the back of his neck being stroked as he bent down. He thought they might be cobwebs and brushed them away but there were no cobwebs to be seen. He often smelt the perfume when he was in the cellar. Before the secret passage had been blocked noises had been heard, not only the clash of swords from the two men fighting the duel, but mysterious footsteps along the secret passage. When the landlord also heard the footsteps he sent his son along to investigate. To his astonishment, the son not only heard the footsteps but actually saw a figure walking ahead of him. It was tall, heavily built and wore a brown curled wig and Regency-style clothes. His footsteps could be heard but they left no trail in the dirt and dust, whereas those of the son were clearly marked.

Each successive landlord over the centuries has heard thumps, noises, voices and clashing swords, all without explanation. A wedding party was disturbed when a glass suddenly hurtled down the table over the heads of the guests. Plates and glasses have smashed by themselves, bottles have burst, and thumps and bangs have been heard in unoccupied rooms, obviously from poltergeists. On 5 July 1963, the *Western Daily Press* published an account by one of its reporters, a Mr Duller, of his personal experiences at the Garrick's Head:

> I can vouch for loud and mysterious bumps in the night. It happened when I was staying in the pub two months ago, *before* I heard the story of the ghosts. Several thuds woke me as I was dozing in the first-floor sitting-room. I searched the room and the corridor outside for ten minutes. But I found nothing except that the sounds seemed to have come from behind the panelling in a corner of the room.

The next morning he told the landlord about his disturbed night and asked what it was all about. The landlord replied:

> I don't believe in ghosts. All the same there's *something*, some funny things going on here. Something grips my arm when I'm pouring out drinks for the customers I'm serving at the bar. Something chipped my car while I was down in the cellar. Something heaved my cash-register, weighing half a hundredweight, off the bar and on to a chair, smashing it to pieces. And that's not all.

In spite of the landlord's disbelief in them they have continued to cause disturbances. Indeed Bath is so proud of its ghosts that 'ghost walks' are frequently organized.

Cornwall: *Dorothy Dingley of Botathan*

Perhaps the most curious ghosts are those tormented and distressed earthbound spirits who can only finally be released in the strange and inexplicable cermony of exorcism by a priest. Such a one was Dorothy Dingley of South Petherwin near Launceston in Cornwall, the central figure in one of the most remarkable of the many hauntings in that county. Her ghost began by terrifying a young boy, then his family, and finally a Launceston priest. Indeed had

it not been for the latter recording in his journal or *Diurnall*,
every detail of the whole sequence of events, nothing
would ever have been known about it.

On 20 June 1665, the Reverend John Ruddle, Vicar of
Altarnun, incumbent of Launceston, later Prebendary of
Exeter, conducted a funeral service in South Petherwin.
After the service he was approached by a Mr Bligh who
seemed very distressed about his son and asked if the
priest could come and visit him the next day and perhaps
help him. As it was Thursday and he had many parish
duties to attend to he promised he would come on the
following Monday.

The Blighs were an ancient and well-connected family,
owning a small but good estate at Botathan, now a farmhouse. Ruddle arrived for an early dinner and was met by
Mr and Mrs Bligh and their son, and another parson.
Almost at once he found Mrs Bligh to be very impatient
about her son's stories of a ghost he had seen several times,
which both she and her husband said was utterly ridicu-
lous. After dinner the other parson invited Ruddle to walk
round the garden, and it was there that he told him the
whole story about the ghost haunting the boy to such an
extent that he was under severe strain, all the more because
his parents mocked and laughed at him and did not believe
a word that he had told them. They thought it was only an
excuse to dodge going to school across the fields to Launceston. Ruddle decided there and then that he would talk to
the boy and he was left alone with him.

Ruddle was immediately convinced of Sam Bligh's truth
and sincerity as he told his story 'with all naked freedom
and a flood of tears'. Sam told him how unjust and unkind
his friends and parents were neither to believe nor pity
him. All he wanted was a man to go with him to the place
where the ghost met him, to be convinced that his story
was real. Ruddle meticulously records the boy's own
words:

This woman which appears to me [saith he] lived a neighbour
here to my father, and died about eight years since; her name,
Dorothy Dingley. She never speaks to me, but passeth by

hastily, and always leaves the footpath to me, and she commonly meets me twice or three times in the breadth of the field.

It was about two months before I took notice of it, and though the shape of the face was in my memory, yet I did not recall the name of the person, but I did suppose it was some woman who lived there about, and had frequent occasion that way. Nor did I imagine anything to the contrary before she began to meet me constantly, morning and evening, and always in the same field (the Higher Brown Quartils), and sometimes twice or thrice in the breadth of it.

The first time I took notice of her was about a year since, and when I first began to suspect it to be a ghost, I had courage enough not to be afraid, but kept it to myself a good while, and only wondered very much about it. I did often speak to it, but never had a word in answer. Then I changed my way, and went to school the under Horse Road, and then she always met me in the narrow lane, between the Quarry Park and the Nursery, which was worse. At length I began to be terrified at it, and prayed continually that God would either free me from it or let me know the meaning of it. Night and day, sleeping and waking, the shape was ever running in my mind, when, by degrees, I grew pensive, inasmuch that it was taken notice of by all our family; whereupon, being urged to it, I told my brother William of it, and he privately acquainted my father and mother, and they kept it to themselves for some time.

The success of this discovery was only this: they did sometimes laugh at me, sometimes chide me, but still commanded me to keep to my school, and put such fopperies out of my head. I did accordingly go to school often, but always met the woman by the way.

Dorothy Dingley, whose ghost the boy knew and recognized, had been often on visits to Botathan, as both families were friends. The Dingleys were an ancient Worcestershire family who had settled in Lezant and Linkinhorne not far away from South Petherwin, so that it was an easy walk. One of her reasons for visiting was Sam Bligh's older brother William. Dorothy was taken ill and died, and was buried in South Petherwin churchyard, the whole

Bligh family attending the funeral service. Some time later William told his family he was going on a visit to London, to which they agreed, but he never returned home.

When the boy had finished his story and Ruddle was in full possession of all the facts they both went out to meet his parents, who at once demanded to know what had transpired. The boy fled to his room but only after Ruddle had arranged that both of them should go early the next morning together to see the ghost and convince the father and mother that there was indeed a ghost. Ruddle again dutifully recorded what happened:

The next morning, before five o'clock, the lad was in my chambers, and very brisk. I arose and went with him. The field he led me to I guessed to be twenty acres, in an open country, and about three furlongs from any house. We went into the field, and had not gone above a third part before the spectrum, in the shape of a woman, with all the circumstances he had described her to me the day before, met us and passed by. I was a little surprised at it, and though I had taken a firm resolution to speak to it, yet I had not the power, nor indeed durst I look back; yet I took care not to show any fear to my pupil and guide, and therefore telling him I was satisfied in the truth of his complaint, we walked to the end of the field and returned, nor did the ghost meet us that time above once.

When they entered the house, Sam's mother asked to see Ruddle privately as she was still anxious and dubious about Sam's conduct, convinced it was some trick to avoid going to school. He told her firmly that her son's story was in no way to be treated lightly. He was satisfied by what he had witnessed, but he reserved his judgement and would carefully consider the case. He warned her not to tell anyone what they had seen together, or rumours would spread round the countryside. He promised that he would return as soon as possible, but he said he had a lot of parish work to attend to, and his wife had been brought home ill from a neighbour's house.

Whatever else he had to do and think about he was

clearly disturbed, not only by the ghost, but by the effect it was having on the young boy. Ruddle must also have wondered about many other points, which though not documented, may be surmised. Why did William go away and never return? Was the ghost at peace as long as he was there but now that he had gone was there a desperate need for Dorothy Dingley to communicate with someone close to him, his brother rather than the parents? Was there something concealed in Dorothy's lifetime which she must reveal? Perhaps she had died in illegitimate childbirth and had never recovered from the shame of it all? And was William perhaps the father of her child?

Three weeks passed before Ruddle returned to South Petherwin, during which time he had pondered deeply on the ghost of Dorothy Dingley. He had made up his mind that before seeing either the boy or his parents he would go alone and see if he could be visited once more by her spirit. On 27 July 1665 he again wrote down in his journal what happened.

> I went to the haunted field by myself, and walked the breadth of the field without any encounter. I returned and took the other walk, and then the spectrum appeared to me, much about the same place where I saw it before, when the young gentleman was with me. In my thoughts it moved swifter than the time before, and about ten feet distant from me on my right hand, insomuch that I had not time to speak, as I had determined with myself beforehand.

That same evening Ruddle went to Botathan to see the Blighs and to persuade them to accompany him to the field, to see for themselves that their son was truthful and had good reason to be terrified at what he had seen. It was with reluctance and after much discussion that they agreed to go. Ruddle warned them solemnly not to breathe a word to anyone about his plan, and if people were suspicious at seeing the family all go out together, to tell anyone they met that they were going to examine one of their fields of wheat to see if the crop was ready to harvest. He himself would go in a different direction and meet them by the first stile. They would meet next morning about the time that Sam was usually on his way to school. He writes:

> Thence we all four walked into the field, and had passed above half the field before the ghost made its appearance, it then came over the stile just before us, and moved with that swiftness, that by the time we had gone six or seven steps, it passed by; I immediately turned my head and ran after it, with the young man by my side; we saw it pass over the stile at which we entered, but no farther. I stepped upon the hedge at one place, he at another, but could discern nothing; whereas I dare aver that the swiftest horse in England could not have conveyed himself out of sight in that short space of time. Two things I observed in this day's appearance, that a spaniel dog who followed the company unregarded did bark and run away as the spectrum passed by, whence tis easy to conclude that twas not our fear or fancy which made the apparition, that the motion of the spectrum was not gradatim, or by steps and moving of the feet, but a kind of gliding as children upon the ice, or a boat down a swift river, which punctually answers the description the ancients give of the motion of their lemures.
>
> But to proceed, this ocular evidence clearly convinced, but withal strangely affrighted the old gentleman and his wife, who knew this Dorothy Dingley in her lifetime, were at her burial, and now plainly saw her features in this apparition. I encouraged them as well as I could, but after this, they went no more.

It was not only the Blighs who were terrified at what they had seen and swore they would never go to the field again, but Ruddle himself had been once again deeply moved and more puzzled than ever. He racked his brain for some solution to what was a very great problem, since the state of the ghost seemed to be desperately in need of some spiritual help he felt only a priest could give to bring peace and rest to her unhappy spirit. He hid all his thought from the Blighs and spent a bad, sleepless night, until at 5 o'clock he rose and crept silently out of the house, determined once again to go and meet the ghost alone.

Soon after five I stepped over the stile into the disturbed field, and had not gone above thirty or forty paces before the ghost appeared at the farther stile. I spake to it with a loud voice, whereupon it approached, but slowly, and when I came near it moved not. I spake again, and it answered, in a voice neither very audible nor intelligible. I was not in the least terrified, and therefore persisted until it spake again and gave me satisfaction. But the work could not be finished at this time; wherefore the same evening, an hour after sunset, it met me again near the same place, and after a few words on each side it quickly vanished, and neither doth appear since, nor ever will to any man's disturbance. The discourse in the morning lasted about a quarter of an hour.

What happened at those meetings will never be known, for Ruddle stated that a binding promise was given on both sides that the facts that Dorothy's ghost confessed to him was not only secret, but some form of 'sin' given in confession to a priest for absolution. There have been wild statements by one writer that Ruddle had studied black magic, that he had gone to meet her armed with a rowan crotched stick to warn off evil spirits or witchcraft, that he drew a circle in the grass with it and spoke to her in the secret Syriac language.

That some form of exorcism was given by Ruddle is certain since her ghost has never been seen again in Botathan or anywhere else in Cornwall. As in so many narrations of ghost stories there are extensive areas for speculation. In this particular case, from start to finish of Ruddle's personal entry into the Bligh family and Dorothy Dingley's ghost, he has meticulously recorded every incident, however trivial, in a determination to solve her problem. He finished his journal or *Diurnall*, as it was called, with utter conviction and truth which leaves no doubt.

These things are true, and I know them to be so, with as much certainty as eyes and ears can give me; and until I can be persuaded that my senses do deceive me about their proper object, and by that persuasion deprive myself of the strongest inducement to believe the Christian religion, I must and will assert that these things in this paper are true.

Devon: The Watching Ghosts of Berry Pomeroy Castle

To come upon the splendid and secluded ruins of Berry Pomeroy Castle, two-and-a-half miles from the fine old town of Totnes in Devon, is both an adventure and an unforgettable experience. It is reached down a long winding glen banked high on either side with shrubs and trees, and its sudden appearance is at first startling and then exciting. Its impressive fourteenth-century gatehouse with its two forty-foot-high flanking towers, its massive curtain walls, and its portcullis grooves projecting round St Margaret's Tower at the end of the ramparts to the right, is as fine an example of medieval architecture to be seen anywhere in England.

It is indeed remarkable that during nine centuries the castle has been occupied by only two families, the powerful de la Pomerais and the Seymours, ghosts of both families haunting the castle. The earliest is that of Henry de Pomeroy who in 1194 sided with John Lackland, later King John, against his brother Richard Coeur de Lion in a treacherous rebellion whilst the king was away on the Third Crusade.

When news came of the king's return to England and that he was setting out to attack Berry Pomeroy Castle, Henry, after assigning all his lands and possessions to his son, ordered his horse to be brought to him blindfolded, then mounting it he rode straight at the north wall and over it in a death-leap. Through the centuries people have continuously reported that on certain evenings as dusk was falling they have seen the blindfolded horse galloping headlong over the wall and heard the shouts of the rider urging it on.

But it is the ghost in and around St Margaret's Tower that is even more terrifying and has more often been seen. It is that of a young woman. In long flowing robes she walks from the tower along the ramparted curtain wall to the room above the Gate House. All who have seen her say she pauses and beckons to them in an urgent way. Her name is Margaret and the tower is named after her. It is said that some three or more centuries ago, when one of the feudal barons de la Pomerai was fighting abroad, he left his elder daughter Eleanor as mistress of the castle. Margaret was Eleanor's younger sister, and in the absence of the strict vigilance of their father they fell in love with the same man. In her jealous rage of her sister's greater beauty Eleanor trapped Margaret in the dungeon below the tower bearing her name, and left her to starve to death. It is small wonder, therefore, that her poor unhappy ghost beckons so vainly for help.

Berry Pomeroy has two other ghosts and one of them the incarnation of evil. It has been said by many visitors that the atmosphere in and around the castle is indefinably haunting, and most especially by St Margaret's Tower, which has strangely affected children playing near it so that they have run away to another part of the profusely scattered ivy-clad ruins. It is in the great courtyard, however, where the sense of being watched is most strong, although over two-and-a-half centuries have passed since the castle was occupied. One stands there dwarfed by the tall and perilous-looking ruins of the towers, walls and ramparts, which originally enclosed it. Rooms with fire-blackened, empty fireplaces stand roofless. Below, to the north, runs a little tributary of the River Dart which once filled the great surrounding moat. It can be seen and heard through the dense forest of trees growing up to and over the walls. Dominating all are the splendid ruins of the great Tudor mansion built within the castle itself in the sixteenth century.

The gaunt stone mullions which once held fine armorial

glass windows, the empty and abandoned series of rooms, the Great Hall, huge fireplaces, all stand open to the sky, wind and rain as they have since a terrible fire razed the mansion to the ground. In all that ruined splendour is still reflected its former dignity and beauty which the passing centuries have mellowed and softened and which, more than any other part of the castle, gives one this strange sense of being watched as one moves from one part to another through the grass and weeds and rubble.

Some time towards the end of the eighteenth century it was struck by lightning in a terrible storm which set fire to the roof and caused a very great deal of damage, so much so that the owner at the time decided he would not spend any more money on the place and allowed it to fall into ruin. Some part of it was still habitable in the year 1796, for a Steward was in residence there. It was he who summoned Dr Farquhar to attend to his sick wife.

Dr Walter Farquhar was a most distinguished physician who came from an ancient Scottish family, he was created a Baronet in 1796, and appointed Physician in Ordinary to the Prince Regent. He was having a short holiday at Torquay when he first received a summons from Lord Seymour to come to Berry Pomeroy Castle. The doctor was noted for his skill, his honesty, and above all for his truth. It is because of the latter quality that the whole of the following astonishing ghost story was not only fully documented by him but fully authenticated.

When he arrived at Berry Pomeroy Castle he was at once shown into what was left of the great Seymour mansion. He was requested to take a seat in an outer apartment until the Steward's sick wife could receive him. It was, according to the doctor, a poorly proportioned apartment, richly panelled with black oak. The only light in the room filtered through the panes of a gorgeous armorial window blazing with coats of arms. There was a great fireplace in one corner, dark open steps formed part of a staircase leading to some room above. 'These steps were touched by the last gleams of a summer's twilight,' he wrote.

As the minutes passed he began to be annoyed at the

delay, for as an eminent physician he was not accustomed to be kept waiting by even his most important patients. Just at the moment when he was considering returning to Torquay, a young woman, richly and exquisitely dressed, entered the apartment. The doctor, sure now she had come to summon him, rose to meet her. To his astonishment she crossed the room with quick steps, wringing her hands in great anguish, passing him by without even glancing at him. She paused for a moment at the foot of the stairs and began to climb them in haste and agitation.

The doctor, following her with his eyes, saw her reach the top stair and pause again. The light falling across her young and very beautiful face plainly accentuated the combination of vice and despair he saw in her countenance. As he later recorded in his memoirs:

> If ever human face exhibited agony and remorse; if ever eye, that index of the soul, portrayed anguish uncheered by hope, and suffering without interval; if ever features betrayed that within the wearer's bosom there dwelt a hell, those features and that being were then present to me.

At the very moment she vanished from sight the doctor was summoned to his patient's bedside by her husband, the Steward, who had entered the room unheard by the doctor. He found the lady very ill, indeed so ill that she required all his skill and undivided attention, so that he completely forgot all about the lady he had seen on the stairs. He said he would have to visit her the next morning and departed. On his return call, he found his patient very much better, which both surprised and gladdened him. When he and the Steward were out of the room he casually mentioned the richly dressed lady, enquiring who she was. To his surprise he saw the face of the Steward blanch with shock and fear. 'My poor wife! My poor wife!' he muttered.

'Why, how does that affect her?' asked the puzzled doctor.

'Much! Much!' replied the Steward emphatically. 'That it should have come to this! I cannot – cannot lose her. You know not the strange, sad history. And his lordship is extremely averse to any allusion being ever made to the circumstance, or any importance attached to it. But I must and will out with it. The figure which you saw is supposed to represent the daughter of a former baron of Berry Pomeroy who bore a child to her own father in that chamber above us, the fruit of their incestuous intercourse. It was strangled by its guilty mother. Whenever death is to visit the inmates of the castle she is seen wending her way to the scene of her crimes with the frenzied gestures you describe. The day my son was drowned she was observed, and now my wife!'

'I assure you she is better,' replied the doctor with conviction and truth. 'The most alarming symptoms have given way, and all immediate danger is at an end.'

The Steward looked despondently and directly at him. 'I have lived in this castle nearly thirty years. I have never known the omen fail.'

'Arguments on omens are absurd,' replied the doctor, somewhat affronted by this challenge to his medical skill and diagnosis. 'A few days will, I trust, verify what I say and see your wife recovered.' He walked to the door and the two men parted mutually dissatisfied. Soon after the doctor's arrival at Torquay a messenger came to say his patient had died at noon.

If Dr Farquhar had been sceptical about ghosts before his visit to Berry Pomeroy Castle, he was sufficiently affected to make some investigations in his own methodical way about the ghost he had seen. He found she was responsible for quite a number of hauntings, always in the same way, but with the addition that she lured anyone who saw her to some unsafe spot in or near the castle which would lead them to a fatal accident. This would, of course, have accounted for the death of the Steward's son who drowned nearby.

Many years passed during which the doctor's fame increased and demands upon him were great. One day a lady called to consult him about her sister whom, she said, was heartbroken, 'overcome and sinking because of a supernatural occurrence in her life'.

'I am well aware of the apparent absurdity of the details I am about to give you, but without them the case will be unintelligible to you.'

She thereupon gave him a full account of a visit she and her brother and sister had made, whilst staying at Torquay, to a place called Pomeroy Castle to see the ruins. To the now plainly startled doctor she went on:

The Steward was very ill at the time of our arrival, I remember this because there was some difficulty in getting the keys to go in. While my brother and I went in search of them my sister was all alone for a few minutes in a large room on the ground floor, and while there a lady passed her in a state of indescribable distress. This spectre, I suppose I must call her, horribly alarmed my sister. Its features and gestures have made an impression on her which time can never efface. We have tried to rally her, to laugh her out of it, but the more we do, the more agitated and upset she becomes. We are most anxious for your opinion and a visit to her without delay.

She paused, anxiously watching the doctor's face. 'You see,' she added, 'when we returned the keys before leaving we were told the Steward had just died.'

The doctor replied: Madam, I will make a point of seeing your sister immediately. But it is no delusion. This I think it proper to state most positively, and previous to my interview with you I myself saw the same figure, under somewhat similar circumstances, and about the same hour of the day. I should very decidedly oppose any raillery or incredulity being expressed on the subject in your sister's presence.

The very next day the doctor visited the sister, and after what must have been a long talk and further medical treatment, she recovered. This very remarkable story was faithfully recorded by Sir Walter Farquhar in his journal, and one cannot possibly doubt any of his statements.

It does not seem at all unnatural then that on a January afternoon, as dusk was falling and we moved through those splendid ruins of Berry Pomeroy Castle, that even without knowing anything about its ghosts, the sense of being watched by unseen eyes was so very strong. The feeling was still further impressed upon the writer by the discovery of three ghosts who never cease to haunt those ruins. So strong are these impressions that he has twice found himself unable to cross through the gatehouse. The most recent visit in April 1987 revealed considerable pre-servation work on the ruins being carried out by English Heritage, but the castle is still owned by His Grace the Duke of Somerset.

Devon: The Ghost House: Sampford Peverell

One of the most vicious ghosts ever to haunt an English house and which took the place over entirely for almost three years, appeared in the large Devon village of Samp-ford Peverell, near Tiverton. It, or they, made life so un-bearable for the new tenants that something had to be done, and not only was the local priest called in to exorcize the house, but as a contrast the governor of the local prison, all to no avail.

From the very beginning of the numerous, strange and frightening events which took place there in the early 19th century, the facts of the case seem hazy, and it was only the fully authenticated and documented narrative which the priest finally published that placed this amongst the more vicious and cruel of ghostly activities.

The 'Ghost House' as it came to be known before, during and long after its occupation, stood at the extreme north-west end of the pretty village of cob-built, whitewashed cottages which had certainly once been used by smugglers evading the revenue men. It had been empty for a long time, and its chances of being let at all by the owner, a Mr Tadley, were considerably diminished by the report of an apprentice that he had not only seen the ghost of a woman flitting about there, but had heard quite frightening noises. Gossip and rumours quickly spread, and few would go near the house in the daytime, and none at all at night.

Thus no one was more surprised and delighted when negotiations to rent the property were advanced by a Mr Chave, who, in the early summer of 1810, came to see it. Whether he had any knowledge of it being haunted and therefore could strike a hard bargain with Mr Tadley, who was prepared to let it go for a peppercorn rent, is not known, though subsequent accusations against both tenant and landlord were given wide publicity, receiving much hostility not only from the villagers but also the neighbouring countryside. However it was, a figure was agreed upon, the tenancy to commence in April.

Mr John Chave brought with him his wife and six servants, five of them named by the local priest in his subsequent narrative. They were Ann Mills, May Dennis, Martha Woodbury, Mrs Pitts and Sally Case. They had no sooner settled in than all hell was let loose, and if Mr Chave had been faintly aware of hauntings when he first began his enquiries about the house and had taken no notice of the gossip, he must certainly have begun to regret becoming a tenant. Some unearthly body, or bodies, at once began rampaging round the house, though invisibly. There were banging doors, beating and stamping on the floors, moving from room to room and back again, upstairs and downstairs, some of the heavy stamping being echoed in another room. The servants felt they were being followed from room to room and heard their own footsteps being echoed. Thunderous noises awoke the whole family from sleep. It was by no means a propitious start for any of them.

The poltergeists, for that they most certainly were, behaved in the way all poltergeists do and have done ever since their activities were first recorded and documented. What is always truly astonishing is how the victims of these malicious spirits continued to submit to their torturers. And secondly, that any head of the family could keep his staff with him, as seemed to happen in the great cases of Hinton Ampner in Hampshire, the Drummer of Tedworth in Wiltshire, and Willington Mill in Northumbria, three of the classic cases of total submission to this peculiar form of persecution. No doubt in those times servants had no option, for without a 'character' as a reference was then called, they had no chance of finding another employer.

The poltergeists, having prepared the ground for their victims, now began to get vicious, beating the maids as they lay terrified in their beds in the one room allotted to women servants. After days and nights of torment and sleeplessness Mr Chave decided to call in the local priest, a Reverend Caleb Colton, to try and drive out the spirits by exorcism. If the reverend gentleman failed in his appointed mission, which he assuredly did, he produced an astonishingly detailed document of every event that took place in the house, more incredible even than the actual events he recorded. It was called *A Plain and Authentic Narrative of the Sampford Ghost*. Later still, when serious accusations were made against him, he added *An Appendix to the Plain and Authentic Narrative* denying the charges. Even later he issued a further pamphlet entitled *Hypocrisy, a Satire*.

Ann Miles was the first one picked out by the ghost for a most vicious attack of beatings on her body as she lay speechless with fear in her bed one night. So severely was she treated that Colton made the first of his many detailed entries. He reported entering the room 'after hearing the terrified screams of all the servants and saw a large swelling on Ann Miles' face as big as a turkey's egg'. As if to placate the suspicion of gossip and rumour-mongers, Ann Miles herself made a voluntary statement on oath to Colton and others, and with truly astonishing *naïveté* declared 'that she was alone in the bed when she received the blows from an invisible hand', evidently the defence of her chastity being more important than the treatment she suffered.

The ghost then switched its attacks to the others, always at night, and always the defenceless women, for it never attacked John Chave. It beat them black and blue to such a degree that they were often unable to work for some days afterwards. Incredible as it seems the sanctimonious reverend gentleman dutifully recorded 'that he had heard upwards of two hundred blows in one night delivered upon a bed; the sounds were like that of a strong man striking with all his might with clenched fists'. It is utterly beyond belief that this man could be somewhere outside the room in which the beatings were taking place, counting the blows carefully, and doing nothing either to call John Chave or go in himself to give any assistance he could to those most unfortunate women. He later wrote of one appalling night of such cruel beatings that they brought shrieks of pain all over the house from those who were being injured: 'The shrieks came from the women who slept in the room, and the symptoms of fear could not be mistaken, a most violent perspiration evinced by large drops standing on their foreheads . . . ', and so on, as if he were actually standing watching them being flagellated and it seems with some masochistic pleasure, unless we gravely wrong him.

That night may well have been the worst, for a surgeon was summoned in the morning and the women swore on oath before him, the Reverend Colton, and another witness, a Mr Sully an excise man, 'that they were beaten so severely they would be numb and sore and unable to work.' Only then did Mrs Chave come into the picture at all, 'allowing them to sleep in the room she shared with her husband.' Even had she not made this singularly generous gesture the servants had already made up their minds they would never sleep in their room again.

But if they were not beaten any more they certainly had no peace, for they were all awakened in the middle of the night by the noise of a large, heavy candlestick moving about. When Mr Chave got out of bed to ring a bell for help, presumably to call for the Reverend Colton, the candlestick hurled itself towards Mr Chave, missing his head by a fraction. Then, when they had once more settled down, the bed curtains of the four-poster bed in which Mr Chave and his wife lay began to move, or, as the Reverend Colton wrote ' . . . being violently agitated with a loud and almost indescribable motion of the rings. These curtains, four in number, were, to prevent motion, often tied up each in one large knot. Every curtain of that bed was agitated, and the knots thrown and whirled about with such rapidity that it would have been unpleasant to be within the sphere of their action. This lasted about two minutes and concluded with a noise resembling the tearing of linen. Upon examination a rent was found across the grain of a strong new cotton curtain.'

Then other new sounds came into the house, something like a man's slippered foot coming downstairs and passing right through the wall. 'I have been in the act of opening a door,' wrote Colton, 'when a violent rapping was heard on the other side of the same door, yet I could swear no one was there.' And again: 'I have been in one of the rooms that has a large modern window, when from the noises, knockings, blows on the bed, and rattling of the curtains I did really begin to think the whole chamber was falling in. Mr Taylor was sitting in the chair the whole time.'

Still no move was made by the Chave family to vacate the house, though a very thorough investigation of every room, beams, walls, floorboards, doors and windows was made. For some reason, perhaps because he was able to control violent prisoners, Mr Searle, the Governor of the county gaol was called in to sit up at night with another independent witness and make their own personal investigations. With yet another totally incongruous and inexplicable action in the wholly mystifying narrative, they placed a sword at the foot of one bed, with a heavy Bible laid upon the bed itself, presumably another of the reverend gentleman's suggestions. To their astonishment and great fear, however, they had no sooner done this than both sword and Bible leapt into the air and dashed themselves against the further wall. Mr Taylor, a friend of Colton who had been present at the earlier incident with the door-rapping, hearing a great noise and commotion, hurried into the room, only to see the sword suspended in the air, its blade pointing towards him, before it clattered to the floor.

By now the continual disturbances in the 'Ghost House', the treatment of the servants, the apparently callous conduct of Mr Chave and the imbecilities of the priest aroused the whole village to great anger. John Chave became their butt, accusations were made against him that he was a trickster, that he caused the mischief by some occult power he possessed in order to buy a house so haunted that it could never be leased to anyone else if he quitted. He was physically attacked by the villagers and by people in Tiverton, some five miles or so away, who though remote from all that was going on had no intention of going near the 'Ghost House'. Other people believed it was Mr Tadley who was trying to get rid of Mr Chave. The *Taunton Courier* published vitriolic attacks in their leaders against the Reverend Colton, who denied all charges in his own pamphlets. Finally the editor openly accused Colton of 'fraud, bamboozling and hoodwinking the public.'

The truth is, [replied Colton in a pamphlet] that the slightest shadow of an explanation had not yet been given, and that there exists no grounds even for suspecting anyone since there are some sixty persons involved. The public were given to understand that the disturbances had ceased, whereas it is well known to all in the neighbourhood that they continue with unabating influence to this hour.

We were told, by way of explanation, that the whole affair was a trick of the tenant who wished to purchase the house cheap – the stale solution of all haunted houses. But such an idea never entered his thoughts, even if the present proprietors were able to sell the house but it happens to be entailed. At the very time when this was said all the neighbourhood knew that Mr Chave was unremitting in his exertions to procure another habitation in Sampford, on any terms. And, to confirm this, these disturbances have at length obliged the whole family to make up their minds to quit the premises, at a very great loss and inconvenience. If these nocturnal and diurnal visitations are the effect of a plot, the agents are marvellously secret and indefatigable.

The Chave family had at last cleared out of the haunted house, unable to stand any longer the pressures of evil spirits which had tormented them for the best part of three years. It is only incredible that they stayed as long as they did, or that none of them had a complete and permanent breakdown of health, or become insane as might conceivably have happened.

It was over two years before Colton came out with a very important statement, which must have silenced most of his accusers. 'I may now inform the public, what the newspapers would not, or could not; namely, that a reward of £250 has been offered for anyone who can give such information as may lead to a discovery. Nearly two years have elapsed and no claimant has appeared. I myself, who have been abused as the dupe at one time, and the promotor of the affair at another, was the first to come forward with £100, and the late mayor of Tiverton has now an instrument in his hands empowering him to call on me for the payment of that sum to anyone who can explain the cause of the phenomena.'

But no one ever did, or has done since. Strangely enough the 'Ghost House' did receive another tenant, a grocer and general dealer, but, far from ever seeing or hearing any ghosts he flatly refused to believe there ever had been any.

One account that smugglers had used Sampford Peverell to hide their kegs of illicit brandy, which they brought by night on pack-horses from as far away as Beer and Seaton seems unlikely. Much later, however, when alterations were made to the house, double walls with passages between were found, a system often used by smugglers to hide their booty, purposefully creating noise to frighten people out of the house. This could well support the account of the noises, but could not explain the beatings, the sword and Bible, and the heavy candlestick. For many years, Colton's narrative and local gossip brought sightseers to Sampford Peverell to stare at the haunted house, even as late as 1876.

But where did those vicious spirits all go? Why did they pick on the unfortunate servants? And why did they never torment the grocer? And will the £100 ever be claimed? The best ghost stories are never solved.

Dorset: *A Suicide Ghost at Eastbury*

In 1717 Sir John Vanbrugh started building the magnificent house of Eastbury within a splendid park in the Dorset village of Tarrant Gunville for George Dodington. By the time the house was finished in 1738 it had cost £140,000, an enormous sum of money even in those days. No expense was spared and most of it, according to rumour, was obtained by illegal means from the Admiralty where he was employed. Three years later, in 1720, he died leaving his estate and £30,000 to his nephew George Bubb Dodington, a flamboyant and highly eccentric son of a Weymouth apothecary, who was later elevated to the peerage as Baron Melcombe of Melcombe Regis.

George Bubb Dodington was even more of a spendthrift than his uncle and squandered money so rapidly that by 1738 he had spent enormous sums on the building, which eventually cost twice as much as it cost Vanbrugh to build his other two great houses, Blenheim Palace and Castle Howard. After Lord Melcombe's death it was sold to the Duke of Buckingham and it was demolished twenty years later, only one wing remains standing today. For the forty years that Melcombe lived there he entertained in ostentatious pomp. He had an enormous portico of columns built as an entrance for visitors wishing to see him. They could only approach him through whole suites of apartments with lavishly painted ceilings and walls hung with velvet. He slept in a specially-made huge four-poster bed canopied with peacock feathers and had an equally large wardrobe filled with the most expensive suits. In addition to Eastbury he had a large and splendid villa in London at Hammersmith which was named La Trappe.

The cost of running Eastbury increased more and more as it grew larger. In the end it became so expensive that even Melcombe could no longer afford to maintain it and actually offered £200 a year and free residence to anyone willing to run it. There were no offers once any applicant had been shown over the house.

Lord Melcombe had a fraudulent steward called William Doggett, known to locals as 'Old Doggett', who had a reputation for being light-fingered, especially during the long absences of his Lordship whilst the building continued. It is his gruesome ghost that has haunted both house and park since he died, particularly the road and the long drive up from the park gates to the house. Doggett made himself conspicuous by wearing breeches tied with yellow silk ribbons, but many of the neighbours thought him a crafty customer and were surprised that he was employed by Lord Melcombe. Their suspicions were not groundless as it proved.

William had a brother who was in serious financial difficulties and who to avoid bankruptcy appealed to him for help. Doggett assisted by illegally selling much of the building material ordered by his master lying all round the house. It became such an easy way of stealing that he increased it daily, probably moving it at night, or even paying one of the workmen to do so on the side, passing the money, (or perhaps only part of it) on to his brother, so that each had a large slice of a rich cake. Doggett reckoned that he could repay the money to his master when he next returned, Melcombe always announcing this decision before he did so. He had been away quite a time, though Doggett had no knowledge of his whereabouts, when suddenly, without any warning at all, Lord Melcombe's coach arrived at Eastbury.

Doggett was in a panic; the amount he owed was very considerable and he knew that his Lordship would soon find out from the invoices and bills awaiting him what material he had or had not, for which Doggett, as steward, was responsible. Without a word to his master, Doggett went into his room and shot himself. It is said that the blood from his body left a stain on the floor which could never be removed. He was buried in Tarrant Gunville churchyard.

Almost at once he began to haunt the house and park in a very strange and gruesome manner that seems inexplicable, more so because a suicide ghost is rarely found in ghost histories. On the stroke of midnight he is often seen on the road waiting to be picked up by a coach with a headless coachman and headless horses. The horses are whipped up and driven to the entrance to Eastbury. His ghost walks straight through all the many suites to his own room where he shoots himself again and vanishes. At other times he has been seen walking in the park or being driven in a coach-and-four. The reason for him always being headless has never been understood. It is known to be Doggett's ghost by his breeches. Even after Eastbury fell into ruin, except for the one wing which was let out as tenements for the labourers, it was not free of his ghost. Strange noises have been heard at night, doors have opened and closed and his ghost has been seen moving about the building and through the rooms.

At one time there were people who did not believe the story, or that there was such a person at all, or that he was buried in the churchyard. The last doubt was removed when workmen rebuilding part of the church of St Mary in Tarrant Gunville in 1845 exhumed the skeleton of a man whose legs were tied together with a yellow silk ribbon, the material not having decayed almost a century after Doggett died, a few years before Lord Melcombe, who died on 28 July 1762. Melcombe was unmarried and the title became extinct.

There was one more incredible story told by local people when Doggett's skeleton was discovered. They said he was a vampire, and this together with the story of his headless body and the blood-stained floor of the room where he shot himself, makes him a rare ghost indeed.

Somerset: *The Sexton and the Rings of Watchet*

Kentsford Manor near the fifteenth-century church of St Decuman on a little hill outside Watchet, was once the original house of the distinguished Wyndham family, many of whom are buried in the church, their monuments being in the Wyndham chapel. One of the brasses there is to Florence, wife of John Wyndham and it is her strange story and her ghost that has for centuries haunted Kentsford Manor. She was taken ill one day and rapidly grew worse, finally dying and her body being buried in the family vault.

The sexton had noticed that her fingers bore valuable rings so he made up his mind there and then that he would remove them for himself rather than the body-snatchers who, at that period, plundered corpses for sale to the hospitals. Waiting until nightfall he entered the vault and began to ease the seven rings from the dead lady's fingers, but one of them cut his finger. His blood spurted out and at the same time he saw there was blood coming from the cut on the finger of the corpse he was robbing. His fear and alarm increased wildly when he saw the corpse move slightly, then rise up in her coffin.

Terrified, he rushed out of the church towards the sea and drowned himself. Florence Wyndham got out of her coffin and walked back to the manor to join her husband again. Even recently her white ghost has been heard tapping insistently and continually on the window-panes of the manor house as if imploring someone to let her in. She has also been seen standing on the staircase.

There is a second local but unauthenticated version of this story, which still involves the sexton. He had set out at about midnight to steal the rings when he was waylaid and set upon by a gang of local ruffians, quite probably body-snatchers who had learned of the death of a rich woman almost certainly buried with her jewellery; it was likely to be a very rewarding raid. They at once ordered him to let them into the church and show them the coffin which he was forced to do by fear of severe injury, even death. When he led them to the coffin, they ordered him to take off the rings and hand them over, snatching them from him, before rushing out of the church.

In the dark church the frightened sexton was even more

terrified when he saw white figures flitting around him. The lady from whom he had stolen the rings sat up in her coffin and at the same time other coffins opened. In absolute panic he fled back to his home. The next day he sent for the rector, protesting his innocence and relating what had happened, but not confessing what his own intentions had been. So deep was the shock that he died that same day.

Somerset: *The Wilful Skull of Chilton Cantelo*

In the north transept of St James' Church in Chilton Cantelo, not far from Yeovil, is the tomb of a very strange man indeed. The inscription on his tomb reads: 'Here lyeth the Body of Theophilus Broome, of the Broomes of the house of Woodlowes neare Warwick town in the county of Warwick, who deceased the 18th August 1670 aged 69. A man just in his actions; true to his friends; forgave those that wronged him, and dyed in peace.'

Whether he died in peace is quite unpredictable for his choice and manner of death was by no means normal, for his deathbed request was that his skull should remain permanently in the house where his sister lived and to which he came after the Civil Wars had ended and the Restoration of Charles II had at last been achieved. That he was a Royalist is evident from the arms on his tomb – *Sable, on a chevron argent three sprigs of Broom proper*. So shocked was he by the bloodthirsty acts he had seen carried out by the Royalist troops that like so many others during those wars he defected to the Roundheads. All his life he was haunted by the atrocities he had witnessed by the Royalists who had hanged, drawn and quartered their prisoners and stuck their severed heads on railings and spikes for all to see.

Thus it was that his deathbed plea to his sister was made that his head should be separated from his body, so that if ever his body were dug up they would find no head to impale and that his skull should never leave the house, a request his sister dutifully had arranged to be fulfilled.

During the years after his death there had been a constant change of tenants, quite possibly due to the skull, for every time it was removed horrid noises took place in protest at its removal. Skulls – often screaming skulls – have played a large part in the history and folklore of ghosts and almost without fail they resist tenaciously any attempt to remove them from where they have always been, almost as if they are quite certain that the body to which they once belonged will be joined to them once more. Thus it was that successive tenants of Higher Chilton Farm had to make their choice between peace and quiet in the house or horrible noises if the skull was moved.

However, one tenant who had had enough of its presence decided on a final attempt to be rid of it, in spite of the warning the outgoing tenant had given him. He applied to the church authorities to have the tomb opened in order to put the skull back with Theophilus Broome's skeleton and thus secure peace at last for both the skull and himself and family. In spite of gaining permission and ordering the sexton to proceed with the work, it ended even more disastrously and inexplicably, for the sexton's spade broke in half, an omen which he was so convinced boded no good to him that he refused to go on with the task. He vowed it was a judgment on him for interfering with the dead, so once again the skull returned to its home and presumably there was peace, at least for a time.

In 1826, however, when alterations and repairs were carried out on the farmhouse, the workmen quite without malice or ill-doing, found the skull in the cabinet and used it as a drinking-vessel when they made tea or drank beer. Perhaps Broome would have been highly amused at this familiarity as long as the skull remained in the house, and was returned to the cabinet.

The skull is now at peace if the body is not, for it rests in a special cabinet with Mr and Mrs Kerton of Higher Farm, Chilton Cantelo, opposite the church. When my wife and I recently visited them about the skull, which we saw in its special place in the cabinet opposite the front door, they said that nothing would ever persuade them to have its peace disturbed in any way and indeed they were grateful to it in a very special way. Before their marriage, Mrs Kerton had visited the house one night and was perturbed at having to live with a skull in the house after the marriage. When the time came for her to leave and get into her car, her future husband, seeing a black shadow on the ground, called out to her that she had dropped her coat. The shadow was not her coat but the top of an uncovered well which, had she not paused to turn, she would have fallen into. It was only one of other stories which were good enough reasons for gratitude to the skull of the strange Theophilus Broome.

Somerset: *The Sedgemoor Ghosts*

It is not surprising that after the terrible slaughter at the Battle of Sedgemoor on 6 July 1685 which lasted only a few hours, there should be ghosts galore in that area of Somerset. James, Duke of Monmouth, illegitimate son of Charles II by his first mistress Lucy Walter (who swore to her dying day that their marriage legally took place and that her son should rule England one day) rebelled against King James II, his uncle, to claim his right to the throne. His abortive rebellion was stupendous folly on his part, even though his claim was probably valid, but the result was disastrous for him. His hurriedly raised army, consisting of a motley crew of ragged, untrained, ill-equipped men, the majority of whom were loyal and brave Somerset men, was flung against the highly-trained and well-armed Royalist army; inevitably Monmouth suffered an ignominious defeat. Monmouth fled, disguised as a shepherd, only to be found hiding in a ditch, captured, sent to London and executed on Tower Hill nine days later. The axe fell several times before he was finally beheaded.

Since those bitter times, the land where the battle took place has been reclaimed, drained and turned into rich farmland, with only a signboard bearing the words 'to the BATTLEFIELD' pointing in its direction. Legend still lingers on in the hearts and minds of the men of Somerset, for it was in their county that Monmouth started and finished his campaign, in their houses that he was given hospitality, rewarding them with personal gifts in return – the feathers in his hat, a gold button cut off his cloak by a bayonet, and most precious of all, a silver buckle with a blue embroidered ribbon given him by his beloved mistress Henrietta Lady Wentworth as a love token, which he always wore round his neck. This he gave to a child whose father had given him hospitality for one night of his flight. He placed it round the child's neck as he kissed him and said, 'This may be of some use to you some day or I can have it again.' It is now in the Blake Museum, Bridgwater, but for countless years after Monmouth's death it was revered by those suffering from scrofula, known as the King's Evil, which could be cured by touching the buckle. Monmouth's ghost and especially the ghosts of his army have passed into Somerset history in legends and folklore.

In the strange, mysterious, haunting countryside of Sedgemoor with its marshes, willows, reeds, dykes and lonely paths across the moors, anything can be imagined without being psychic.

In the daytime, mist shrouds the moors and real figures seem to be ghosts, and even more so as night begins to fall and silence is over the whole countryside. Is it then not feasible that people have reported the sight of phantoms, apparitions, horsemen and armed soldiers suddenly bringing fear as they appear out of the mist and disappear as quickly as they came?

Just over fifty years ago, a London journalist travelling at midnight on one of the lonely moorland roads, across which slowly drifted thick mist, suddenly braked hard as he nearly hit a man mounted on a big horse just in front of him. The journalist, calling out a greeting, began to move slowly past the horseman who was staring straight ahead of him as he rode, and did not answer. The journalist suddenly became aware that there was no sound of the horse's hooves on the road. Then in a flash the horseman bounded forward, jumped a bridge and vanished. Frightened by this experience, the journalist stopped as the mist drifted across and cleared, but there was no sight of a bridge or the horseman and he had no doubt at all that he had seen a ghost.

But it is on the anniversary night of 6 July when Monmouth's ranks broke and scattered that Somerset folk have seen Monmouth's ghost, cloaked and furiously riding from the battlefield. People have even waited to see him, singly or in twos and threes, to bear witness that they told truth. They have seen armed and unarmed soldiers in flight, actually identifying the weapons and the uniforms.

An even more piteous story is that of the White Lady who haunts the Sedgemoor gravemound, a pathetic figure wringing her hands and wailing, lifting her arms above her head, finally prostrating herself bitterly weeping across the gravemound. Her lover had been the champion runner of Sedgemoor and had joined Monmouth's army, but was captured by the Royalists. When he told them of his running feats they put him to the test, promising him his liberty if he proved his boast was true. They haltered him naked to a wild moorland pony to see if he could outpace it. He managed to cover more than three-quarters of a mile at an incredible speed before collapsing with exhaustion and bleeding feet, but the jeering soldiers hanged him just the same. The White Lady lost her reason and would not leave the gravemound, dying there of her grief.

There are a great number of haunted places in Somerset; numerically Sedgemoor has the most. Bussex Rhine is one place (rhine being a Somerset word for ditch or dyke). Before the battle a gypsy had given Monmouth a warning saying, 'Beware of the rhine', but he did not understand because he thought she meant the German river, so he took no heed. The nearby Bussex Tree was where the champion runner was hanged.

Yet another haunted place is at a crossroad on the Stogursey-Bridgwater road where the ghost of a constantly wandering red-coated soldier was seen. He was probably a deserter from the Royalist army. When workmen were ordered to put up a signpost a shallow grave was discovered containing a skeleton and remnants of red cloth, but since the skeleton was removed the ghost has not since been seen.

Hoddon Oak, until it was cut down in 1979, was where six rebels were hanged in chains, one from each of the surrounding villages, and it was said that moans and clanking of chains were heard when people passed in daytime, not daring to do so at night. But the most frequent and more dreaded ghost was in Taunton, that of the 'Bloody' Judge Jeffreys, the villainous, merciless and ruthless hanging judge of the Monmouth rebels after their defeat, perpetrator of a calendar of appalling cruelty unequalled in English history. His pilgrimage of hangings in chains is terrible to read and Somerset was the main centre for the trials, sentences of death or transportation were automatically passed on the rebels. Indeed his room at the Tudor Tavern is said to be haunted merely by the fact that he sat there and his bewigged ghost has been seen in the castle museum waiting on a landing, for Monmouth and his army occupied the castle.

It was once written of Jeffreys, 'The Lord Chief Justice breathed death like a destroying angel and sanguined his very ermine with blood'. Not only did he pass the death sentence but added that the culprits should be hanged in chains, be drawn, quartered, their bodies disembowelled, their limbs burnt in pitch and their hearts plucked out of their bodies. His western circuit covered Dorset, Devon and Somerset, where in the great hall of Taunton Castle and the Assizes in Wells he dealt out his evil punishments which Somerset people have never forgotten to the present day. The two worst places were Ilminster and Taunton, but it was in Taunton that the most terrible executions took place on the gibbets, on the site of the present Market House, then called Cornhill, to which the prisoners were brought from Bridewell. Near to the gibbets a great fire was kept going so that the prisoners could see where their entrails and limbs would be burned after quartering.

In the horrific gaol of Ilminster over four hundred rebels were herded together like sheep, in filth and darkness, their wounds festering and undressed, awaiting transportation or their journey to the gibbets of Taunton. To get there they were either thrown into carts or, if walking wounded, chained like slaves together and marched beside the carts, prodded on by the swords of the Royalist escort.

One of the most wanted men the Royalists sought was Plomley of Locking Manor, near Weston-super-Mare, the rich local squire who, before becoming a high-ranking officer in Monmouth's army, had hidden all his treasure in a well in the grounds. After the defeat he fled as fast as he could, knowing full well what his fate would be if caught. He hid for some time in the Cheddar caves, themselves haunted, and when he thought the coast would be clear, returned to the Manor. In spite of evading capture on the way, he was finally cornered and a detachment of soldiers was sent to bring him back dead or alive. In the nick of time he escaped to Locking Woods and hid there in a coppice, known to this day as Plomley's Coppice, while the soldiers ransacked the house for the treasure.

Throughout the ordeal, his wife held their spaniel in her arms who was whimpering and struggling to get at the soldiers. The search went on until, at the moment of leaving the house in a complete state of disarray, the spaniel struggled free from his mistress' arms and rushed out to the woods where he had often seen his master, barking so loudly and with such enthusiasm that the suspicious soldiers immediately rushed towards the dog, found their victim and dragged him out. Both the dog and Plomley's wife were taken to Taunton where she was forced to watch her husband being hanged, drawn and quartered. One of their sons was taken prisoner and another was hanged.

After this, the wife was allowed to return home and the first thing she did was to take the excited spaniel into her

arms, rush to the well where the treasure and her own
jewels were hidden, and fling herself and the dog down it.
Ever since that time, over three hundred years ago, her
ghost has been seen and heard restlessly moving towards
the house, clutching in her arms the little dog who had so
innocently betrayed her husband. With so many hauntings
in their county how can the people of Somerset ever cease
to believe in ghosts?

7 Scotland

Angus: The Drum of Death: Cortachy Castle

Cortachy Castle, home of the distinguished family of Ogilvy, Earls of Airlie, has for long been haunted by a ghostly drummer. To hear his drum beating a tattoo is always a death-warning to the family, though often it has been a friend or guest who has first heard it round the castle walls.

The castle, an ancient fortress, stands in the wilder part of Angus, one of many, each having its own peculiar legends and ghosts, though few as sinister as the Airlie drummer. A former minister, who wrote a history of the family, has fully documented the story of the drummer. He has also personally testified to the fear and dread members of the family feel when told of the drum beats.

The family of Ogilvy goes back to the twelfth century, when Scotland was ruled by King David, and Gilbride was 1st Earl of Angus. In 1492 Sir James Ogilvy was created 1st Lord Ogilvy of Airlie. Some two hundred years later they were created Earls of Airlie as a reward for their loyalty to Charles I. James, eldest son of the first Earl, was taken prisoner, sentenced to death, but disguised in his sister's clothes escaped the very night before his execution. In spite of being attainted, the honours were restored to the family after a long period of time.

It was during those troubled times that the other castle belonging to the family, the fifteenth-century Airlie Castle, was looted and burned down whilst the Earl was absent. It was the scene of further action during the Jacobite Rebellions of 1715 and 1745, when Lord Ogilvy fled to France.

The castle was restored in 1792, and in 1961, after it had been used as a Dower House for seventy years, became the home of the 11th Earl of Airlie. In 1963, Angus Ogilvy, brother of the present earl, married Princess Alexandra, one of the most popular marriages of this century, the couple being greatly loved and respected by the people.

There are two versions of the actual origin of the ghostly drummer of Airlie. One is that he was the bearer of an unpleasant message from another clan chieftain. In those times it was a common thing for a messenger bringing bad news to be forced to eat the message he brought, both the parchment on which it was written and the wax seal upon it. If he managed to survive after this most unappetizing meal, he was often killed anyway.

Drummers were quite frequently sent as messengers and it was not unknown for a violent-tempered recipient of the message brought to him to force the drummer to eat part of the parchment of his own drum. He was then taken to the battlements, his broken drum rammed down over his head, and his body flung to the courtyard below where, with luck, he was able to die. The first version says that the Airlie drummer was one of those who brought a message of ill omen to Cortachy Castle.

The second version is different, perhaps more probable, and certainly more plausible. As was customary in those days the clan chieftains had their own private retinue of soldiers and servants, amongst whom was always a drummer. The Airlie drummer was, it is recorded, a young and very handsome one. The maidservants, and even the guests who visited the castle found it impossible to resist both his smile and his charm. This, very naturally, did not take long to create dissension and jealousy among the female staff, and quarrels soon broke out amongst the jealous ones. It was not long, consequently, before the matter was brought to the notice of the earl himself.

It may well be he had his own private views about the whole business, since his wife was very young and also very beautiful. He at once angrily summoned the drummer to be brought before him. He not only warned him of his behaviour but threatened him with the severest punishment if he continued to pursue the women as he did. For a time there was peace, but soon the drummer was at work again. Once more he was summoned before the earl, who angrily told him he would have him put to death if he did not cease his pursuits. In those days all clan chieftains exercised their right to administer capital punishment within their own territories, actually continued by one of them as late as the early nineteenth century.

A most violent quarrel broke out between the drummer and his lord. The drummer even dared to tell the earl that if he carried out his threat of death he, the drummer, would haunt his fa.nily and the castle for evermore. It may well be the earl had his own private fears of such a threat being carried out, or that he was even more jealous and suspicious of his wife than before, but it was not long before he acted. One night shortly after the quarrel he and some of his men discovered the drummer in a room at the top of the castle where he had no right to be, likely enough with one of the women. They rushed in, dragged him out, bound his hands and feet together before carrying him to the topmost tower of the castle. There they rammed his drum right down over his head and flung him headlong to the courtyard below, where he instantly died. From that very moment almost, and true to his prophecy, the ghostly drum has been heard and always it has brought death to a member of the family.

No actual period of time has been recorded when the drummer's vicious sentence was carried out, but in the year 1844 something very strange indeed happened at Cortachy Castle. The event was documented in detail, proving without any doubt that the drummer had not made his threat in vain. One evening of that year, at Christmas time, a certain Miss Dalrymple, related to the Earl of Stair, was staying at Cortachy Castle as the guest of the 6th (9th allowing for attainder) Earl of Airlie. Whilst she was in her room dressing for dinner she suddenly heard the sounds of music coming up from the courtyard below. As she went to the window and pulled the curtains to see who was playing, the music faded and became dominated by the beating of a tattoo on a drum. It had a hollow note which she suddenly and unaccountably felt to be eerie and disturbing, so much so that she rang for her maid to ask her who the drummer was. The maid's face visibly paled as she was asked the question before awkwardly replying that she knew nothing at all about a drummer and that she herself had heard nothing. Miss Dalrymple thereupon continued her dressing, for the drum had stopped playing, and she put the matter out of her mind until she went down to dinner.

It was some time during the meal that Miss Dalrymple, obviously still puzzled about the music and the maid's confusion, suddenly said to her host; 'My lord, who is your drummer whom I heard under my window while I was dressing?' The earl at once turned very pale, staring in astonishment and anxiety at his guest. The silence that had fallen over the whole table could almost be heard, and it was plainly seen by everyone round the table that the countess was even paler than her husband. Almost everyone in the room had heard the question and most of them knew the grim legend.

Miss Dalrymple's own embarrassment was acute, and she, like everyone else, was relieved when someone started to talk again and break the heavy silence. But everyone there could see the terrible distress and fear on the faces of the earl and countess. When the countess rose from the table, preceding the women guests to the drawing-room and leaving the men over their glasses of port, Miss Dalrymple, acutely aware now of her unconscious error, said to Miss Ogilvy, who was a close friend, 'I seem to have made a very bad *faux pas*. What is the mystery? Why did both Lord and Lady Airlie look so pale? Who is this drummer?'

'What, have you never heard of the drummer boy here?' asked Miss Ogilvy.

'No!' answered the even more puzzled Miss Dalrymple. 'How should I? Who then is he?'

'Why,' answered Miss Ogilvy, 'he is a ghost who goes

about the house playing his drum whenever there is to be a death in the family. The last time he was heard was shortly before the death of the earl's first wife. That is why he turned so pale just now. It is a very unpleasant subject in this family, I can tell you.'

This information embarrassed and depressed Miss Dalrymple even more than before, and she was already seeking a reasonable excuse for leaving the castle as soon as courtesy permitted when she went up to her room that night to sleep. She could not have known that within a few hours, as she was dressing before breakfast, she would hear the drum again, beating its tattoo below her window overlooking the courtyard. She at once informed the earl she would have to leave sooner than she thought, not daring to say she had heard the death-warning again, and that she must leave as soon as possible that morning.

Within six months the countess, the earl's second wife, died whilst on a visit to Brighton. After her death a paper was found on her desk on which she had written that the conviction that the drummer had beaten his drum for her had preyed much upon her mind and undoubtedly hastened her end. The extraordinary thing about it all is that only Miss Dalrymple had heard the ghost drummer. It seemed as if this had become his method of passing on the message, perhaps to make confusion worse confounded. This was proved four years later, in 1849.

It was on 19 August in that year that a young Englishman had been invited to stay at Cortachy Castle for a shooting party. He set off on his pony one morning, accompanied by a ghillie to Tulchan Lodge, a shooting lodge out in the wilder Forfarshire countryside. The going was not easy through the tough heather and across the frequent burns, and had it not been for the ghillie's knowledge of the moors the Englishman would very certainly have lost his way. After some three or four hours they reached the shooting box, had an hour or two of grouse shooting, and set off back to the castle.

It began to grow darker as the hours passed. The journey had been long, since some twenty miles or more separated the Tulchan from Cortachy, but as it now began to grow really dark they could see the castle lights twinkling ahead of them. As they drew nearer to the castle the Englishman was suddenly surprised, and then delighted, to hear music from a distance. The music grew louder the nearer they came to the castle, until it was very loud indeed, dominated by the roll of a tattoo on a drum. Then the music ceased and only the regular beating on the drum could be heard, strangely and indefinably sinister.

'What is it, Donald?' he asked the ghillie. 'That music, what is it? There surely can't be a band outside the castle at this time of night? And who is the drummer?'

'Ah canna hear nothing,' the ghillie answered sullenly. 'There's nae band. There's nae drummer. It'll be the wind.'

'Nonsense, man,' said the Englishman. 'I heard it as plain as a pikestaff.'

'Well if ye heard it at all it's no canny,' growled the ghillie. He drove his pony forward, not stopping until both of them reached the castle entrance where the ghillie, with a gruff 'good-night', rode away to the stables.

As the young Englishman entered the castle he was informed that Lord Ogilvy had been summoned to London where his father was dangerously ill. The very next morning the earl died.

This seems to have been the last time that the drummer was heard, but the fear of his death warning is still very much the concern of the family. As the Reverend John Strachan, minister of the Established Church at Cortachy wrote, 'The legend is no longer believed in, but superstition dies very hard.'

Perthshire: The House of Terror: Ballechin House

The dramatic and frightening number of ghosts who ruled for so long, and so tyrannously, over the great Scottish mansion of Ballechin House have probably caused more controversy than any other case in the country, excepting perhaps Borley Rectory in Essex.

The great, rambling, sixteenth-century mansion of Ballechin House is at Strathtay, near Dunkeld in Perthshire. It was occupied by the Stewart family for some four hundred years, during which time everything in the occult and supernatural world seems to have taken place there. All the most thorough and painstaking investigations of the leading psychic experts of the time proved fruitless, and the coincidences between that house and Borley Rectory are in themselves very remarkable.

The dates of mounting interest in the activities of the ghosts were progressive. In 1892 a Jesuit priest had a bad time with them. In 1893 he met another lady who had suffered from their attacks. In 1896 the ghosts were highly active, aggressive and vicious. In the year 1897, and for a whole month, *The Times* printed all the letters which poured into the office in response to the first one sent to them by the butler of Ballechin House, which set a match to the gunpowder barrel.

As a result of all these letters, John, 3rd Marquis of Bute, himself deeply interested in the occult and supernatural world, made a determined effort to deal with the situation. He had done nothing since he had heard from the Jesuit priest, Father Haydon, who first gave him a detailed explanation of what he had endured five years previously when a guest in Ballechin House. The priest had heard rumours that it was haunted but disregarded them, as he did not believe in anything supernatural. He had not even minded when he was put into one of the reputedly haunted rooms because the others were occupied.

I went to Ballechin on Thursday, July 14, 1892 [he recorded] and I left it on Saturday, July 23, so I slept at Ballechin for nine nights, or rather ONE night, because I was disturbed by very queer and extraordinary noises every night except the last, which I spent in Mr Stewart's dressing room. At first I occupied the room to the extreme right of the landing, then my things were removed to another room. In both these rooms I heard the loud and inexplicable noises every night. In addition to those another noise affrighted me – a sound of somebody or something falling against the door outside. It seemed at the time as if a calf or big dog would make such a noise. Why those particular animals came into my mind I cannot tell. But in attempting to describe these indescribable phenomena I notice I always do say it was like a calf or big dog falling against the door. Why did I not hear the noises on the ninth night? Were there none where I was? These are questions to which the answers are not apparent. It may be there *were* noises but I slept too soundly to hear them . . . (1) It seemed to me that somebody was relieved by my departure. (2) That nobody could induce me to pass another night there, at all events.

This reference to a big dog could be a key point in the case. Between the years 1834 and 1876 the house was occupied by Major Stewart. When he died he was succeeded by his sister Mary's second son, who assumed the name of Stewart. Major Stewart, or 'the old Major' as he was called, not only believed deeply in the supernatural but many times convincingly told all who knew him that he would return to life after death in the form of his favourite black spaniel. He had a passion for dogs, possessing some fourteen of them at the time of his death, but the black spaniel was his favourite and went with him everywhere so that they were inseparable.

After his death the prospect of 'the old Major' returning to his former home as a black spaniel produced nothing but anxiety and fear amongst his relatives. The heir's first decision, therefore, was to shoot all the dogs. This he promptly did, but if he thought such drastic measures would have any effect upon the ghosts already there he was wrong. They appeared in greater strength even than before and almost immediately after the post-mortem which was necessary following 'the old Major's' death. In spite of the fact that every effort was made by the domestic staff to eradicate by whatever means the smell of dogs from the house, it constantly came at odd moments of the day, and most especially in 'the old Major's' study, where it was quite overpowering. It was very apparent whenever the heir's wife was in there attending to the household accounts. Often she felt heavy pushes against her legs as of a big dog bumping against her. In spite of the fact that she had no belief whatsoever in spirits she began to feel disturbed whenever she entered the room.

A year after Father Haydon's unpleasant experiences at Ballechin House he met, quite by chance, a young woman who had once been a governess there for some twelve years. Without telling her anything at all of his own disturbances, merely saying he had stayed there, she told him how the hauntings had become so bad that she was forced to give up her job and leave. She added that the worst room was the Blue Room, which was where Father Haydon had himself slept. Very many haunted houses have a Blue Room, quite frequently the scene of murders and evil spirits.

That same year was a highly eventful one for two reasons. The first was the singular death of the Stewart heir. One day, prior to his departure for London he was talking to his agent, when suddenly the conversation was interrupted by three distinct, very loud raps. Though no believer in ghosts himself Stewart was nevertheless disturbed, perhaps remembering his ruthless massacre of the dogs. He concealed his feelings, however, and set out on his journey. Almost immediately on his arrival in London, he was knocked down by a passing cab and killed. When the news was told to the Marquis of Bute he said the three loud knocks had been a warning of ill omen sent by the spirits.

Shortly after this Ballechin House, together with the shooting, was let for twelve months to a wealthy Spanish family. Such were the hauntings that they were driven out only eleven weeks later, counting the cost of a rent forfeiture of nine months as cheap in exchange for freedom from fear. It was their butler who wrote the first letter to *The Times* which triggered off all the successive events and expert investigations.

He wrote of rattling doors, knockings, stampings, 'tremendous thumpings' on doors, heavy footsteps echoing along the passages. All his statements were corroborated by guests and servants alike who were too terrified to stay there any longer. 'For the two months I was there,' he wrote, 'and almost nightly, every visitor that came to the house was disturbed. Sometimes the whole house was aroused. One night I remember five gentlemen meeting at the top of the stairs in their nightshirts, some with sticks or pokers, one with a revolver, all vowing vengeance on the disturbers of their sleep'.

The butler then went on to record his own vigils, alone or with others, to try and solve the mystery. On three different nights his bed-clothes were torn off him, or lifted off his body, first at the foot and then at the head of his bed. In spite of clutching them he felt invisible hands touching his own and forcing him to release his grip. There was a fanning round his head as of the wings of a great bird flying round the room. Then both he and his bed were lifted up and dragged across the room to the window. Every single event which took place in the house was always preceded by heavy knocking on the doors.

'As I heard the clock strike two a crashing vibrating batter struck against the door where my sister was sleeping', he wrote. This was the same noise the Jesuit father heard, describing it as of a calf or dog being hurled against the door. The knockings increased in number, often six now, and with more and more violence, night after night. The guests and staff continued to leave so that only the family remained, though their decision to go as soon as possible had already been discussed. It became positive when the first piercing shrieks echoed through the house and aroused everyone. The next day they left.

All these events finally prompted the Marquis of Bute to act personally in the matter of Ballechin House. He therefore consulted with the two greatest living psychic experts,

Colonel Lemesurier Taylor and Miss A. Goodrich-Freer. It was decided to rent the house for three months in the name of Miss Freer. She would take up residence there with Colonel Taylor and a friend, Miss Constance Moore, daughter of the Prebendary of St Paul's Cathedral and Chaplain to Queen Victoria.

On 3 February 1897 they took over the house, engaging a staff of servants from Edinburgh. In order to conceal the real motive thirty-five guests were invited to a country house-party as it was called. No one was given the slightest suspicion that the house was haunted or that investigations were to be carried out. It was felt that observations could be made more easily this way than for the experts to go there alone and thus highlight what they were doing. Also it would be of the utmost value to collate any evidence of hauntings by guests simply out to enjoy themselves and probably much more receptive to any unusual happenings. Every single detail of this experiment was carefully documented by Miss Freer and Lord Bute in a book they later published entitled *The Alleged Haunting of B— House*. It aroused so much interest that the book ran into a second edition as late as 1900.

Almost from the moment the experts, guests and staff entered the house the spirits really got to work; all they had previously done seemed to be quite insignificant. In the very early morning of the first day after Miss Freer's arrival she was suddenly awakened by a terrific noise. It echoed all through the house, sounding like someone beating a clanging metal bar with a hammer. This went on for two hours until about 4.30, when mysterious voices were distinctly heard on the same floor. Her frightened maid later told her she too had heard the voices, and also a sound of heavy furniture being dragged and banged about in one of the rooms.

On the next night the maid again heard strange noises, the oddest of which was the voice of someone reading aloud, or so it seemed to her since it was continuous, unbroken by the intrusion of another voice as in a normal conversation. It was more like a monk or priest saying his office or telling his beads. A new kitchen maid who had been engaged that day refused to stay the night, leaving before 11.30, having heard more than enough from the others.

Nor were any of the unsuspecting guests immune from manifestations, for if none of them believed in ghosts when they arrived they certainly did when they departed. The nightly visitations increased. Doors were beaten upon so violently that the whole house was awakened. There were distinct footsteps heard in locked and empty rooms, voices raised angrily by an invisible man and woman in one of the corridors, other strange voices, shuffling footsteps, dragging of heavy furniture, rappings, and clanging noises. Even the dogs the guests had brought with them reacted sharply, often anticipating some of the disturbances seconds before they occurred.

Then the first of two really unnerving experiences came to two of the guests when they were passed on the staircase by the figure of a hunchback who glided silently between them. The second encounter was even more unnerving for another guest. His hobby was photography and one day he was setting up his camera in one of the rooms when he suddenly felt, and then saw, a large black spaniel in the room. He took little notice until his own dog, also a black spaniel, came rushing in, wagging its tail and chasing away the phantom one. It would seem, therefore, that 'the old Major', true to his promise, had come back to the house after death in the manner and form he said that he would.

It also began a whole series of 'doggy' incidents. Other guests felt themselves pushed or touched by what could only be the bodies of dogs. They suddenly smelt them in rooms where no dogs were, or had been. They heard distinct rappings on doors as if made by a dog wagging its tail. Then one night two ladies who shared a room were suddenly awakened by the whimperings of their pet dog who always slept on one of the beds. One of the ladies lay terrified at the sight of two black paws of a bodyless and headless dog on a bedside table, which suddenly vanished. When yet another guest was scared out of his life as he awoke from sleep by the sight of a detached hand holding a crucifix, Miss Freer decided to hold a séance and consult the spirits themselves.

She therefore assembled all those remaining guests who, surprisingly enough, continued to stay on in the house, and all sat down with an Ouija board. This was a form of planchette used to communicate with troublesome spirits. In answer to questions she put, automatic writing appeared, a phenomenon not unknown to spiritualists. One of the questions she asked was the name of the lady portrayed in the oil painting which hung in the hall and who was dressed in what appeared to be eighteenth-century costume. The writing produced two names, 'Ishbel' and Margharaed', which were Gaelic for Isabel and Margaret. After a pause the writing began again, telling Miss Freer 'to go at dusk to a glen in the garden up by the burn'. The communicating spirit said her name was Isabel, and she repeated the name several times in emphasis.

Miss Freer obeyed these instructions as soon as she could, and has herself documented in her book what she saw, 'Against the snow I saw a slight, black figure of a woman moving slowly up the glen. She stopped, turned, and looked at me. She was dressed as a nun. Her face looked pale. I saw her hands in the folds of her habit. Then she moved on, as it seemed, on a slope too steep for walking. When she came under the tree she disappeared.' After this quiet though disturbing experience she saw the nun often. 'Once she was in tears. Her weeping seemed to me passionate and unrestrained.'

With her usual thoroughness Miss Freer at once studied the family history more closely, discovering that a sister of 'the old Major' became a nun and died in 1880. Miss Freer then rightly or wrongly assumed her to be Isabel. The nun was seen only by Miss Freer, and always in the same spot in the glen. On another day, however, two nuns were seen in the grounds by two ladies whose dog, a very quiet animal, actually ran barking towards them before they vanished. No ghost of a nun was ever seen in the house.

At the end of the three months of her investigations Miss

Freer left, but two other experts arrived. They were Mr
F.W.H. Myers and Professor Oliver Lodge, the latter of
whom wrote to Lord Bute, 'We have not heard the loud
bangs as yet. Knocks on the wall, a sawing noise, a droning
and a wailing are all we have heard.' In another letter to
Miss Freer he wrote, 'There has been nothing for me to do
here as a physicist, and I return home tomorrow. Nevertheless, the phenomena, taken as a whole, have been most
interesting . . . some of the raps seemed intelligent.'

It was a rather cold dismissal of the power of those spirits
who had caused only fear and alarm during the whole time
they occupied Ballechin House. The case is surely one of
the most puzzling in the very considerable and varied
history of ghosts. In spite of every kind of investigation
nothing was ever solved. The ghosts, presumably satisfied
when the last of the occupants left, took over again, and
perhaps in a much quieter way since there was no one left
to drive away.

The fully documented report which Miss Freer collated,
and in conjunction with the Marquis of Bute, published in
a book, did not appear until two years later. By then the
storm first raised by *The Times* correspondence had blown
itself out and no one at all seemed to be interested in what
had been at one time a very remarkable case indeed,
though interest later awakened.

Yet there was a very strange, ironical sequel to it all
when, much later, Jesuit priests were called in by a new
owner to exorcize the place. All of them saw only one ghost
and that one never seen before, not even by the vigilant
Miss Freer. It was the ghost of a parson, and of the opposite
faith, so who exorcized whom in the end?

8 Wales

Gwent: The Troubled Spirit of Tintern Abbey

In a loop of the River Wye some ten miles downstream from Symond's Yat, are the splendidly impressive ruins of Tintern Abbey in its lovely setting. In the reign of Henry II, a colony of Norman monks began to lay the foundations. They came from L'Aumone, an offshoot of the fine monastery of Citeaux in France. These were the great years of monastery, convent and abbey buildings in England, possessing all the qualities of which the monks were so conscious; remoteness of position for peace and quiet, and always near water for the abundance of fish they required.

Tintern Abbey was occupied by the Cistercian order who wore white habits and were known as the white monks, so hated by King John because of their wealth and great lands. After the Dissolution of the Monasteries by Henry VIII, Tintern gradually fell into the fine ruins visible today. Had a friend of Lord Halifax not told him of a strange supernatural experience he and his wife had had, a story which he published in his own book entitled *Lord Halifax's Ghost Book*, there would have been no record of what is perhaps the oldest ghost of all, the troubled spirit of Tintern Abbey.

The narrator of this story and his wife were on a bicycling tour in the spring of 1895 and had reached Tintern Abbey. They were so enchanted with what they saw that they decided to spend two days there. After dinner they went to look at the Abbey and were immediately enchanted by the mystery and beauty of the ruins as they wandered about them. Impelled by what he saw and knowing her psychic

171

gifts, he asked his wife if she felt as deeply moved as he did, and if so could she use her rare and wonderful gift of automatic writing entirely directed by a spirit. She replied that she did and both of them sat down on a block of masonry as she drew out her writing pad and pencil. Within seconds her right hand began moving by some invisible power which rapped repeatedly on her knee with a force she was powerless to resist, even had she wished to do so.

The husband then suggested to her to ask the spirit to moderate its force and give three taps for 'yes' and two taps for 'no' to any questions they might ask when it had communicated with them. Her hand rose at once then lowering it gently to her pad she gave three very slow taps.

> We then established communication by the tedious but usual process of going through the alphabet until a tap announced the right letter had been reached. Many questions and answers resulted until we received information.

The personality in control then told them that he was a soldier of Saxon descent serving under Henry II. The husband at once queried this since no Saxon would ever have served under a Norman king. Nevertheless, answered the Saxon soldier, he was telling the truth. He then went on to say that he had fallen in battle in the neighbourhood of the Abbey but had been buried near without any prayers being said over his body, and he could not rest. He told them that he knew he was neither good nor bad nor was not altogether unhappy in his present state, but he could not rest until a Mass had been said for his soul, when everything would be at peace and he would ask for nothing more. The husband then asked him why after the lapse of centuries he should apply to two Anglicans, as he and his wife were, and whose church did not include prayers for the dead as part of their doctrine.

The Saxon soldier said he had tried in vain all through the centuries to communicate with someone to ask this favour but without success, but now that he had he would be inexpressibly relieved if they could help him. When they promised that they would try and do something, he said he would be most grateful and bade them goodnight. The release of the lady's arm by the ghost was effected and the two strolled back to bed, filled with mystery and wonder at what had happened to them.

The husband remembered that he had a friend a Father A— who might be able to arrange a Mass for the unquiet soldier and sat down at once to write to him, posting the letter the next morning on their way to the Abbey once again, but nothing occurred. As they were leaving Tintern early the next morning they decided to return to the Abbey that night after dinner. Once again the Saxon soldier took control of the wife's arm and the soldier was asked if there was anything else they could do for him, but he said what they had done already was good and he was very grateful. He only needed a Mass to give him rest and he would never again trouble anyone. Then the control ceased, the wife's arm was released and they left the Abbey for the last time.

On their return to London there was a letter awaiting them, asking the husband to make an appointment to see Father A—. This he did and explained to him the whole story. The priest informed him that his church gave him full power to say Masses for the unknown departed and this he would do, promising to say four Masses for such an unquiet spirit.

A year later Father A— died, but in 1905 a strange reminder was given that his promise had been fulfilled. At a séance in the couple's home two of the ladies attending were known to be psychic; one was a very old friend, the other a new acquaintance. The husband recorded:

We sat down. It was not quite dark, for the fire was burning. At first a number of messages from acquaintances who had passed away were delivered in the usual way by raps or the tilting of the table until the power seemed to be exhausted and the manifestations ceased. Thereupon our new acquaintance grew impatient and pressed with some heat for further messages to be given. My wife protested, pointing out that we should not try to force the power whatever it might be, it should be treated with courtesy. The table immediately tilted towards her and slowly tapped out the words 'Very many thanks'. We thought she was being thanked for her remonstrance, but the taps continued. The whole message was 'Very many thanks for the Masses said'. Afterwards the two psychic ladies who were sitting on either side of my wife had seen standing behind her the bearded figure of a handsome middle-aged man, dressed in strange close-fitting clothes of a grey material.

This was the strange story told to Lord Halifax and so far as can be traced there has never been, before or since, a recorded communication between a visitor to Tintern Abbey and that unquiet Saxon soldier, so that at last, after many centuries of patience, he rests in peace.

Powys: The Ghost's Reward: Powis Castle

Many are the legends and ghost stories connected with the grim red sandstone medieval fortress of Powis Castle, near Welshpool in Wales. Of them all, the most singular and the most authentic is the incident which took place in the Haunted Room, so meticulously recorded in 1780 by the well-known Wesleyan Methodist preacher John Hampson.

Powis Castle commands the upper end of the Severn valley, and has been in the Herbert family, the Earls of Pembroke, for centuries. The castle was bought in 1587 by Sir Edward Herbert, son of the first Earl of Pembroke. Sir Edward's son, William, was created Baron Powis in 1629 and fought for the king in the Civil Wars, the castle falling to the Parliamentarians in 1629. The third Baron Powis was elevated first to an Earldom and then became a Marquess. He was sent to the Tower on suspicion of being in the Popish Plot. On his release he fled the country out of loyalty to James II. Soon after his wife smuggled the Prince of Wales, later 'The Old Pretender', to Versailles, where he became the guest of Louis XIV.

The exiled king created the Marquess a Duke, but the title was not recognized in England. In 1784 the Herberts married into the Clive of India family, and for nearly a century took the family name of Clive, though in 1807 it reverted again to Herbert. Powis Castle is now vested in the National Trust and open to the public. Its gardens are superb and Admiral Rodney, whose monument is there, always insisted on his ships being built from the great Powis oaks.

When John Hampson first heard of the local poor woman who had not only actually seen but exchanged a long conversation with the legendary ghost of Powis Castle, he was sufficiently interested to examine her personally. His task was made easier by the fact that the woman herself 'had become serious under his ministry'. Strangely enough he does not reveal her name, though everyone for miles around knew both it and the story, the details of which had spread like wildfire through the surrounding countryside, most especially because of its remarkably mysterious ending.

This woman had always been poor, earning what little she could by spinning hemp and flax. It was customary for the local farmers, and even the gentry, to grow enough of both these plants for home consumption. It was because she was proverbially good at her spinning that she was always welcome at the houses. In return for her spinning, they provided her with board and lodging during her stay, giving her a small additional present of money when she left to go to her next place.

One day by chance she called at Castell Coch, or Red Castle, as Powis Castle was always called, enquiring if there were any work for her there. She was told that the Earl of Powis and his family were away in London, but the Steward's wife said she herself had a considerable amount of spinning she wished to have done and invited her in. As it was early in the morning she was shown to a room where the hemp, flax, and spinning-wheel were kept, and set to work at once. As evening drew on, the Steward's wife said that as there was still a lot of work to do she should stay the night, continuing the next morning. After supper the

woman, who was now quite tired, said she would like to go
to bed if someone would show her the room she was to
have. The Steward's wife rang for a servant to give her the
orders. In a few moments not one but three servants, each
carrying a lighted candle in her hand, preceded the woman
to her room.

She quite expected to go upstairs to the customary attic at
the top of the house where the staff all slept. Instead, to her
great surprise, she was escorted to an apartment on the
ground floor. It had a boarded floor, two sash windows,
was superbly furnished, and contained a great four-poster
bed. Someone had already made up the fire, which burned
brightly in the grate. Before it were a handsome chair and
table, on which stood a large lighted candle. So over-
whelmed was she by the grandeur of the room that she
even protested it was much too fine for her as she was used
to living very simply indeed. The servants, however,
insisted that the Steward's wife had ordered this room to
be prepared especially for her, so here she must sleep.
Then, scarcely disguising their haste to be gone, they
moved towards the door, wished the old woman good-
night, and quickly withdrew, pulling the door so tightly
behind them as to hasp the spring-sneck in the heavy brass
lock that was upon it. They knew that this was the legendary Haunted Room and that the Steward's wife had deliberately designed to test the truth of the story of the castle
ghost by putting that simple woman there to see if she
would be visited at all and what would happen.

The old woman, still dumbfounded at being left in such a
room, which she felt sure was meant only for 'quality'
people, as the gentry were called locally, was almost afraid
to sleep in that enormous bed. She took out her few simple
things, and as she always read a chapter of the Bible before
going to sleep, she sat down at the table in front of the fire
and took out her precious Welsh Bible. After reading her
chapter it was her custom to kneel and say her prayers
before climbing into bed to sleep. As she now sat quietly
reading, her lips silently spelling out the words to herself,
she heard a sound. Looking up and towards the door she
saw, to her surprise and even slight fear, a gentleman

standing in the doorway. He was splendidly dressed in a
gold-laced suit and hat. After a slight pause he walked to
the second of the sash windows in the corner of the room,
before returning to the first window he had passed. There
he stood, resting his elbow on the sill, his chin held reflec-
tively in the palm of his hand, gazing into the distance and
darkness.

The old lady, unable to speak so great was her astonishment, watched him closely and nervously, sure that he
must be one of the 'quality' who had not gone to London
with the rest of the family, and that she was an intruder in
his own private room. He seemed to be waiting for her to
speak, but she dared not utter a word, even if she had been
able to do so. He was standing in such a position that she
could see his profile clearly. She noticed his handsome,
aristocratic features, which confirmed even more her conviction that he was of 'quality'. Then suddenly he turned
round, walked towards the door, paused a moment,
opened it, then closed it after himself, just as the servants
had done.

She was now very alarmed indeed. She wanted to ring
for the servants but felt it presumptuous to do so. In any
case they may well have gone to bed. She felt positive that
the figure she had seen must have been some sort of a
ghost, and then it suddenly struck her that she had been
put in the legendary Haunted Room that was so much
talked about in all the villages and houses. No wonder they
had put her in such a grand room. It was to deceive her, to
see how she, a poor God-fearing woman, would deal with a
ghost. She did not know what to do, dared not call for help,
dared not leave the room, since the whole house would be
in darkness and she had no knowledge at all of the passages
or many other rooms. In fear and much anxiety she took up
her Bible again, then clasping it in her hands she moved
towards the great bed and knelt down, beginning to pray
earnestly for help and guidance. She had scarcely begun
her prayers when the figure silently entered the room
again, walked all round it, then stood behind her. She was
now so terrified that she could not even pray, kneeling
there and unable to move any part of her body. Then once

again the apparition walked out of the room, closing the door behind him just as he had done the first time.

She tried hard to pray again, begging God most earnestly to calm her fear, to give her strength to deal with whatever this restless spirit wanted her to do. Then a third time it returned, walked round the room as before and stood behind her again. As she told John Hampson later, it was her appeal for help to God which suddenly gave her the strength and will-power to deal with the spirit. She turned her head, saw it standing there watching her, then struggled from her knees to face it.

'Pray sir,' she said, 'who are you and what do you want?'

The ghost slowly raised its arm and held out its hand towards her as it spoke.

'Take up the candle and follow me and I will tell you who I am.'

Obediently, and now strangely less afraid, she took up the big candle the servants had put on the table for her, following the figure out of the room. It led her along what seemed to be an endless corridor, the candle-light sending their shadows leaping about the walls and ceilings. At last they reached a door which the spirit opened, beckoning her in to what was a very small room indeed, more like a closet. She hesitated about entering but he simply spoke to her in a gentle voice.

'Walk in. I will not hurt you.'

It had not occurred to her until that moment that he might have hurt her. He had frightened, disturbed, and alarmed her certainly, but not hurt her. She walked in and he at once closed the door behind them both.

'Observe what I do, will you?' he asked.

'I will,' she answered.

He stooped to the floor and tore up one of the boards. She saw that some way down there was an object which looked like a large tin box with an iron handle on the lid and obviously quite heavy.

'Do you see that box?' he asked.

She nodded, alert with curiosity now and no longer afraid.

'Yes I do,' she answered.

He then moved to one side of the room and pointed out to her a small crevice in the wall. 'The key to the box is hidden there,' he said. 'Both box and key must be taken out and sent to the Earl in London'. He then named the Earl and gave her the address of his London house, to which he had gone.

'Will you see that that is done?' he asked.

'I will do my very best to get it done,' answered the woman sincerely.

'Do so, and I will trouble this house no more.' The strange figure then walked out of the room and left her alone.

Once more all her fear returned and moving towards the door she began to beat on it and to shout, her cries echoing all over the house. In a few minutes, the Steward, his wife, and some servants came running from all parts of the house to where she was standing. The servants were clinging to one another and carrying lights that wavered in their shaking hands and caused their shadows to leap across the walls and ceilings, frightening them even more. None of them dared tell the woman of the plot, and how they had all waited to see if the legendary ghost would appear to her and what it would do. Questions came from all sides, but it was some time before the poor woman could babble out her story coherently and in detail, as she tried to recall it all.

After a little more time and further questions by the Steward she showed him where the key was hidden, and where the box was, but he refused to touch it. His wife, however, was determined to obey the ghost's instructions for fear of the Earl's displeasure if she did not, and together with the servants tugged and pulled at the very heavy box buried under the floorboards until they managed to drag it up and into the room.

Neither she nor her husband dared open it to examine its contents, so she ordered the servants to carry it downstairs, keeping the key herself until arrangements could be made to send the box to the Earl's London residence. Then every-one went back to their rooms to sleep, certain at last there would be peace in the house, not only that night but for ever, if the ghost's instructions were carried out.

The next morning the box, key, and a letter from the Steward explaining everything, were sent off, and all waited to hear what the Earl would say and do when he received it. They had not long to wait for as soon after its arrival as possible an express messenger came from London to the castle with sealed instructions for the Steward.

The Earl informed him that such was his gratitude towards the poor woman who had been visited by the ghost and had seen its wishes carried out, that she could, if she wished, reside in the castle as his guest for the rest of her life, without having to work any more. If, however, for her own personal reasons she preferred to live elsewhere, she would still receive an allowance liberal enough to cover all her worldly needs and keep her from working. He would express his gratitude to her personally when he arrived back at the castle. Naturally the Steward obeyed his master's instructions at once, and John Hampson confirmed that the Earl carried out his promise to the full.

It has never been disclosed what the contents of the heavy tin box were, though they were obviously of very considerable importance to the Earl himself. From the very night the ghost left the old woman with his secret and his promise he never returned. So peace at last came to Powis Castle and has remained there ever since.

Principal Sources

Aubrey, J., *Miscellanies*, 1696

———, *Brief Lives*, 1949

Baring-Gould, S., *Cornish characters and strange events*, 1935

Braddock, J., *Haunted houses*, 1986

Briggs, K.M. and Tongue, R.L., *Folktales of England*

Burke, C., *Shropshire folklore*, 1883

Collinson, J., *History of Somerset*, 1791

Colton, Rev. C., *Narrative of the Sampford ghost*, 1810

Crowe, C., *The night side of Nature*, 1848

Curtis, C. *Sedgemoor and the Bloody Assizes*, 1930

Dale, Owen E., *Footfalls on the boundary of another world*, 1859

Day, J. W., *A ghost hunter's guide book*, 1956

Ellis S. M., *Short stories and legends of Berry Pomeroy Castle*

Fox, A., *King Monmouth*, 1902

Halifax, Viscount, *Lord Halifax's Ghost Book*, 1936

Hall, T. H. *New light on old ghosts*, 1965

Hanning, P., *Dictionary of ghosts*, 1982

Hardwick, C., *Traditions, Superstitions and Folklore*, 1872

Harland, J. and Wilkinson, T., *Lancashire legends*, 1873

Harman, H., *Sketches of the Bucks. Countryside*, 1934

Harper, C. G., *Haunted houses*, 1924

Hasted, E., *History of Kent*, 1797

Henderson, W. *Notes on the folklore of the Northern Counties of England and the Borders*, 1866

Hole, C., *Traditions and customs of Cheshire*, 1947

———, *Haunted England*, 1940

Hutchinson, W., *History and antiquities of Cumberland*, 1794

Ingram, J., *Haunted houses and family traditions of Great Britain*, 1900

Jarvis, *Accredited ghost stories*, 1823

Johnson, W., *Folk memory*, 1908

Lawrence, B. *Somerset legends*

Lang, A. *Cock Lane and common sense*, 1894

Lee, Dr F. G., *Glimpses of the Supernatural*, 1875

Legg, R., *A guide to Dorset ghosts* (Bournemouth)

Luddom, H. *The mummy of Birchen Bower*, 1966

Maple, E., *The realm of ghosts*, 1964
Marc, A., *Haunted Castles*
Newton, Lady, *The house of Lyme*, 1917
Norman, D., *The stately ghosts of England*, 1963
O'Donnell, E. *Family ghosts and ghostly phenomenon*, 1933
————, *Ghosts of London*, 1932
————, *Haunted Britain* (3rd impression)
————, *Ghost short stories*, 1909
Page, M., *The battle of Sedgemoor*, 1930
Palmer, K., *The folklore of Somerset*
Poole, K. B., *Ghosts of Wessex*
Powley, E. B., *Official guide of Berry Pomeroy Castle* (Totnes)
Price, H., *Poltergeists over England*
Roy, C., *Ghosts and legends*, 1975
Russell, E. *Ghosts*, 1975
Sergeant, P. W., *Historic British ghosts*
Sitwell, S. *Poltergeists*, 1940
Tongue, R. L., *Folklore of Somerset*
Turner, J., *Ghosts of the South West*, 1973
Underwood, P. *A gazetteer of British ghosts*, 1971
————, *Into the occult*, 1972
————, *West country hauntings*, 1986
————, *Haunted London*, 1973

Series covering counties in this book are:
>   *The King's England*: Arthur Mee
>   *Highways and Byways*: various authors
>   *The Buildings of England*: (ed.) Nikolaus Pevsner
>   *Gentleman's Magazine*
>   *Notes and Queries*

Also:
Society for Psychical Research, (especially for Willington Mill and Ballechin House documents and information)
Local historical societies, field clubs, county histories, regional journals and magazines

Acknowledgements

I must express my deep gratitude to many County Libraries, Librarians and Local History Societies for all their help in the writing of this book, especially York, Chester and Derby. I am also indebted to the Incorporated Society for Psychical Research for authenticated and documented photocopies of required material, The *Newbury Weekly News* (*Out and About* magazine), Mr and Mrs Kerton of Higher Farm, Chilton Cantelo, Mrs Farquharson of Eastbury House and Mrs Bellhouse of Chapel-en-le-Frith. It would be impossible for me to omit my inexpressible gratitude to Madeline, my wife, for her patience and unstinted help with the manuscript through the long months of hard work involving research, typing, photography, proofreading and constant checking.

Index

Airlie, Earls of, 157–62
Amphlett, Mrs Margaret, 44,
  46, 49
Andrews, Miles Peter, 47–8
armies, ghostly, 80–3, 152–3
Arthur, King, 82
Assembly Rooms, Bath, 122
Avon ghosts, 118–25
  Bath, 121–5
  Bristol, 118–21

Ballechin House, Perthshire,
  162–70
Barlow, Father Ambrose,
  85–6
Basildon, Berkshire, 28
Bath, 121–5
Berkshire ghosts, 26–9
  Basildon, 28–9
  Bucklebury, 26–8
  Chieveley, 28
  Hampstead Norreys, 28
  Longworth, 28
  Wash Common, 28
Berry Pomeroy Castle, Devon
  132–8
Beswick, Miss, of Birchen
  Bower, 86–91
Birchen Bower, Lancashire,
  86–91
Bligh Family, Botathan, 126–
  30
Blount, Bessie, 73
Blount, Dorothy, 73–5
Blount, Sir George, 73–6
Bolingbroke, Lady, 27
Bolingbroke, Viscount, 27

Botathan, Cornwall, 126–31
Brede Place, Sussex, 112–17
Bristol, 118–21
Broome, Theophilus, 149–51
Brown Lady, of Raynham
  Hall, 19–25
Brown, Robert, 62, 65
Buckinghamshire ghosts,
  29–34
  Creslow, 29–34
Bucklebury, Berkshire, 26–7
Burrow, Dr Ian, 73
Burton Agnes, Yorkshire, 85
Bussex Rhine, Somerset, 153
Bute, John, 3rd Marquis of,
  163, 165–70
butterfly ghost, 123

Cadbury Fort, Somerset, 82
Calverley Hall, Yorkshire,
  96–100
Calverley, Walter, 96–100
Cambridgeshire ghosts,
  13–19
  Sawston Hall, 13–19
CAMPERDOWN, HMS, 35
Castlereagh, Robert Stewart,
  Lord, 79–80
Chave, John, 139–44
Cheshire ghosts, 50–6
  Lyme Park, 50–3
  Thurleston Old Hall, 53–6
Chieveley, Berkshire, 28
Children Family, Ramhurst,
  109–12
Chilton Cantelo, Somerset,
  85, 149–51

Civil War, 28, 149
Cobb Family, Thurleston Old
    Hall, 53–6
Cock Lane, Smithfield, 39–44
Cockpit Steps, St James's
    Park, 37, 39
Coldstream Guards'
    barracks, London, 36–9
Colton, Revd Caleb, 140–44
Corby Castle, Cumbria, 77–9
Cornish ghosts, 125–32
    Botathan, 125–31
Cortachy Castle, Angus,
    157–62
Country Life, 24–5
Creslow Manor,
    Buckinghamshire, 29–34
Crowe, Mrs, 77–9
Cumberland, Duke of, 28
Cumbrian ghosts, 77–83
    Corby Castle, 77–80
    Souter Fell, 80–3

Dalrymple, Miss, 159–61
Dartford, Kent, 47–8
Defoe, Daniel, 42
de Pomeroy Family, 132–6
de Pomeroy, Henry, 132–3
de Pomeroy, Margaret, 133
Derbyshire ghosts, 56–61
    Tunstead Farm, 56–61
Deserted Village, The
    (Goldsmith), 20
Devon ghosts, 132–44
    Berry Pomeroy Castle,
        132–8
    Sampford Peverell, 138–44
'Dickie' (skull), 56–60
Dingley, Dorothy, 125–32
Dixon, Ned, 56–7
Dodington, George (Lord
    Melcombe), 145–7
Doggett, William, 146–7

dogs, ghostly, 164–5, 168
Dorset ghosts, 145–7
    Eastbury, 145–7
Downes Family, Wardley
    Hall, 83–6
Downes, Penelope, 84–5
Downes, Roger, 83–5
Drummer of Death,
    Cortachy, 157–62
Drury, Dr, 94–5

Eastbury House, Dorset,
    145–7
Easton, Reginald, 53–6
Eaton Place, London, 34–5, 36
Elizabeth I, 16–17
Epsom, Surrey, 46–9
Epworth, Lincolnshire, 61–9
exorcism, 125, 131, 170
Eyre, Major Anthony, 14

Farquhar, Dr Walter, 134–6
'Father John', of Brede Place,
    113, 114–15, 116
Findlay, Revd Brian, 72–3
Frazer, Mary, 41, 43
Freer, A. Goodrich, 167–70
Frewen, Captain, 112–13,
    114–15, 117
Frewen, Claire (later
    Sheridan), 115–17
Frewen Family, 112–17
Fryer, Alfred, 57, 58

Garrick's Head Hotel, Bath,
    123–5
Goldsmith, Oliver, 20, 42
Grey, Lady Jane, 13, 15–16
Grey Lady, of Sawston Hall,
    13, 15, 18–19
Grey Lady, of Theatre Royal,
    Bath, 123
Greystoke, Rector of, 77–8

Hallam, Mrs Gordon, 72
Hampshire ghosts, 101–5
  Portsmouth, 101–5
Hampson, John, 174, 175, 180
Hampstead Norreys,
  Berkshire, 28
Harrison, Mr, 103–4
Haydon, Father, 163–4, 165
Head, John, 28
Herbert Family, 174–5,
  179–80
Hill Street, Mayfair, 44–6
Hodden Oak, Somerset, 154
Hogarth, William, 42
Hole, Christina, 53
Hoole, Revd, 65–6
Houghton Hall, Norfolk, 19–
  21
Howe, Admiral, 122
Huddleston, Sir John, 15–16
Huddleston Family, of
  Sawston Hall, 13–19

Ilminster, 154, 155
Ingram, John, 88–9, 90
Ireland, 79–80

Jacobite Rebellion, 1745, 81,
  87, 157
Jeffreys, Judge, 154
Jellicoe, John Rushworth,
  Earl, 36
'Joe at Tanners', 89–90
John, Dr Jeffrey, 70, 72
Johnson, Dr Samuel, 42, 44,
  121–2
Jones, George, 37

Kent ghosts, 105–12
  Dartford, 47–8
  Ramhurst Manor, 105–12
Kentsford Manor, Somerset,
  147–9

Kent, William, 39–43
Kent, William (architect), 20
Kerton, Mr and Mrs, of
  Chilton Cantelo, 150–1
Kinlet, Shropshire, 73–6

Lake District ghosts, 77–83
  Corby Castle, 77–80
  Souter Fell, 80–3
Lancashire ghosts, 83–91
  Birchen Bower, 86–91
  Wardley Hall, 83–6
Lancaster Family, Cumbria,
  81–3
Legh, Sir Percy, 50–2
Legh, Thomas, 51–2
Leoni, Giacomo, 50
Lincolnshire ghosts, 61–9
  Epworth, 61–9
Locking Manor,
  Weston-super-Mare,
  155–6
Lodge, Prof. Oliver, 170
Loftus, Colonel, 21–2
Lomax, Mr, of Tunstall, 57–9
London ghosts, 34–44
  Cock Lane 39–44
  Eaton Place, 34–6
  St James's Park, 36–9
Longworth, Berkshire, 28
Lord Halifax's Ghost Book, 53,
  56, 171–4
Lyme Park, Cheshire, 50–3
Lyttelton, Thomas, Lord, 44–
  9

Magdalen College, Oxford,
  70–3
Manchester, 86–91
Manchester Museum, 86, 87,
  91
Mann, Thomas, 92, 93–4
Markham, Admiral, 35

Marryat, Captain Frederick, 22–4
Marten, Sir Harry, 28
'Marthe' of Brede Place, 112–13, 116
Martindale, Father, 18
Mary, Queen of Scots, 52–3
Mary Tudor, 13, 15–16
Melcombe, George Dodington, Lord, 145–7
Midsummer's Eve, ghostly appearances on, 81–2
Miles, Ann, 139, 140
Monmouth, James, Duke of, 151–2, 153
Moore, Constance, 167
Myers, F.W.H., 170

Neagle, Dame Anna, 123
Nevill, John, 13
Norfolk ghosts, 19–25
    Houghton Hall, 19–21
    Raynham Hall, 19, 21–5
Northumberland, John Dudley, Duke of, 13, 15
Northumbrian ghosts, 91–6
    Willington Mill, 91–6, 139

Ogilvy Family, 157–62
Old Jeffery, of Epworth, 61–9
'Old Nobes', of Basildon, 28–9
Oliphant, Catriona, 71–2
Orford, Robert Walpole, 1st Earl of, 19–20
Orford, 3rd Earl of, 20
Orford, Horace Walpole, 4th Earl of, 20
Owen, Nicholas, 16
Owen, Robert Dale, 105, 110–12
Oxenbridge Family, 113–14, 117

Oxenbridge, Sir Goddard, 114
Oxford 70–3

Parsons, Elizabeth, 40–4
Parsons, Thomas, 39–43
Pembroke, Earls of, 174–5, 179–80
Pit Place, Surrey, 45, 46–9
Plomley Family of Locking Manor, 155–6
poltergeists, 9, 19, 91–6, 123, 124–5, 138–44
Portsmouth, 101–5
Powis Castle, 174–80
Price, Harry, 17–18
Proctor, Joseph, 91–6
Provand, Captain, 24–5

Ramhurst Manor, Kent, 105–12
Raynham Hall, Norfolk, 19, 21–5
Recruit House, St James's, 36–8
Rigby, John, 17
Rochefoucault, François La, 20
Ruddle, Revd John, 126–32

St James's Park, London, 36–9
St John's Church, Clerkenwell, 39, 41, 42, 44
Sampford Peverell, Devon, 138–44
Samwell, Mr, 101–3
Sawston Hall, Cambridgeshire, 13–19
Scottish ghosts, 157–70
    Ballechin House, 162–70
    Cortachy Castle, 157–62

'Scratching Fanny' of Cock
   Lane, 39–44
Sedgemoor, Battle of 151–3
Sedgemoor, White Lady of,
   153
Sheridan, Claire (née
   Frewen), 115–17
Sheridan, Margaret, 115
Shira, Indra, 24–5
Shropshire ghosts, 73–6
   Kinlet, 73–6
skulls, haunted, 56–60, 83–6,
   149–51
Society for Psychical
   Research, 91, 96
Somerset ghosts, 82, 85,
   147–56
   Chilton Cantelo, 85, 149–51
   Kentsford Manor, 147–9
   Sedgemoor, 151–3
Souter Fell, Cumbria, 80–3
South Petherwin, Cornwall,
   125–6, 127, 129
Stewart, Capt. Robert (later
   Lord Castlereagh), 79–80
Stewart Family, of Ballechin
   House, 163–5
Stoke Bishop, Bristol, 118–21
Stone, Lucia, 22
Surrey ghosts, 44–9
   Pit Place, 44–9
Sussex ghosts, 112–17
   Brede Place, 112–17

Taunton, 154–5
Taylor, Col. Lemesurier, 167
Thurleston Old Hall,
   Cheshire, 53–6

Tintern Abbey, 171–4
Townshend, Charles
   ('Turnip'), 20–1
Townshend Family, 20–5
Tryon, Sir George, 34–6
Tunstead Farm, Derbyshire,
   56–60

VICTORIA, HMS, 35–6

Walpole, Dorothy, 19, 20–1,
   25
Walpole, Horace, 20, 42
Walpole, Sir Robert, 19–20
Wardley Hall, Lancashire,
   83–6
Wash Common, Berkshire,
   28
Welsh ghosts, 171–80
   Powis Castle, 174–80
   Tintern Abbey, 171–4
Wesley Family, 61–9
Wesley, John, 61, 62, 63, 69
Wesley, Samuel (father of
   above), 61–2, 63, 65–9
Westcote, Baron, 45
Weston-super-Mare, 155–6
Willington Mill,
   Northumbria, 91–6, 139
Wyndham Family, of
   Kentsford Manor, 148–9

York, 98
York, Duke of, 122
Yorshire ghosts, 85, 96–100
   Calverley, 96–100
York Villa, Bath, 122